Standard Grade Computing

Frank Frame

Heinemann Educational Publishers
Halley Court, Jordan Hill, Oxford OX2 8EJ
Part of Harcourt Education

Heinemann is the registered trademark of
Harcourt Education Limited

First published 2004

08 07 06 05 04
10 9 8 7 6 5 4 3 2 1

British Library Cataloguing in Publication Data is available
from the British Library on request.

ISBN 0 435 4500 7 7

Edited by Roger Parker
Designed by Artistix
Typeset and illustrated by J&L Composition

Original illustrations © Harcourt Education Limited, 2004

Cover design by Wooden Ark

Printed by The Bath Press Ltd

Cover photo: © Getty

Picture research by Peter Morris

Acknowledgements

Every effort has been made to contact copyright holders of material reproduced in this book. Any omissions will be rectified in subsequent printings if notice is given to the publishers.

Photos: Alamy (pages 77, 79 bottom left); Belkin (page 110); BMW (page 79 bottom right); Corbis (pages 68, 123 left)/Steve Chenn (pages 9, 16)/Jim Graigmyle (page 15); Epson (pages 115, 117 both, 138 top); FGE (page 119); FileMaker International Ltd (page 22 top right); Fujitsu (page 107); General Electrics (page 113 left); Hitachi (page 79 top left); Honda (page 75); IBM (pages 113 right, 118 left); Microsoft (page 21 right); NASA (page 78); Psion (pages 118 right, 121); Science Photo Library (pages 82, 123 right); Smart (page 114 bottom); Sun Micro Systems (pages 101, 108, 138 bottom); Techsoft (page 79 top middle); Wacom (pages 79 top right, 114 top).

Screenshots: Yahoo (pages 12 and 13) reproduced by kind permission of Yahoo! Inc. © 2004 by Yahoo! Inc. Yahoo! and the Yahoo! logo are trademarks of Yahoo! Inc. AppleWorks (pages 35 and 36) reproduced by kind permission of Apple Computer Inc. Filemaker Pro (pages 51, 53) reproduced by kind permission of FileMaker International Ltd. Mediator 7 Pro (pages 59 bottom and 62) reproduced by kind permission of Matchware Ltd. Serif DrawPlus 5 (pages 21 left and 24 bottom) and Photoplus 5 (page 54) reproduced by kind permission of Serif (Europe) Ltd. XpertRule Knowledge Builder (page 22 bottom right) reproduced by kind permission of Attar Software Ltd. All other screenshots reproduced by kind permission of Microsoft Corporation.

Contents

Introduction

Computers and related technologies play an increasingly important part in our everyday lives. The Standard Grade Computing qualification is aimed at equipping candidates with problem-solving skills that can be used in a variety of contexts, and providing practical experience in areas where computers are used.

This book is designed to cover the Standard Grade Computing syllabus with the exception of programming – which can be covered using the companion Heinemann textbook entitled *Learning to use Visual Basic* by Abe Holmes. The content of the book covers all Foundation, General and Credit topics and is divided into the following units:

- Unit 1: Communications and networks
- Unit 2: General-purpose packages
- Unit 3: Automated systems
- Unit 4: Computer systems
- Unit 5: Commercial data processing

The book is designed to enable you to work as independently as possible, either in class or at home. It explains all of the topics clearly and has lots of materials to help you through the course.

Features of the book

Throughout the text there are a number of features that are designed to help you extend your learning and relate theory to practical contexts. The features are:

- Now you try
- Next steps
- Knowledge checks
- End of unit progress checks.

Now you try

These are a combination of questions and suggested activities that will help you get to grips with the ideas you have been reading about.

Next steps

This feature contains more in-depth text and activities designed for students aiming towards credit level.

Knowledge checks

These are intended to help you measure your progress during the course. Try to answer them as well as you can. Take your time – there is no time limit involved. You can look back at the pages you have just read to refresh your memory. Remember: if you simply copy out the answers without trying to answer the questions, then you will not really know how well you are progressing.

What if some of your answers are wrong?

If a couple of your answers are wrong then you should copy out the correct answers. If more than half of them are wrong then you should:

- re-read the relevant pages
- copy out the correct answers

Once you have done all of these you should be ready to move on.

End of unit progress checks
These are designed to help you check how well you have done in each unit.

Answers to questions and on-line assessments
You will find the answers to the end of unit progress checks on the Heinemann website at www.heinemann.co.uk/vocational.

Are you using this book in school?
If you are using the book in school your teacher will correct your answers and give you a grade. Your teacher will tell you whether you need to go back and read any part of the notes or attempt any of the questions again.

Are you using this book at home by yourself?
If you are using the book by yourself, you can check your answers on the Heinemann website and then analyse your score by turning to page 167.

Finally, I hope that you enjoy your Standard Grade Computing course and wish you every success in achieving your qualification.

Frank Frame

Unit 1

Communications and networks

What you will learn in this unit

- What is a network?
- Local-area networks (LANs)
- Wide-area networks (WANs)
- E-mail
- The Internet
- What you can do using the Internet
- Social, legal and ethical issues

What is a network?

A network is a series of computers linked together so that they can send and receive data. Computer networks are great fun and very useful.

You can use a network to send and receive mail, swap sound files, gather information, listen to the radio, watch TV, get money out of your bank, get information for your school projects, buy CDs and book your holiday. You use networks all the time. It's time to find out a little more about them.

Local-area networks (LANs)

Local-area networks are limited to one building or site. The computers are linked together by cables or wireless connections (Figure 1.1). Schools, factories, universities and businesses have their own LANs.

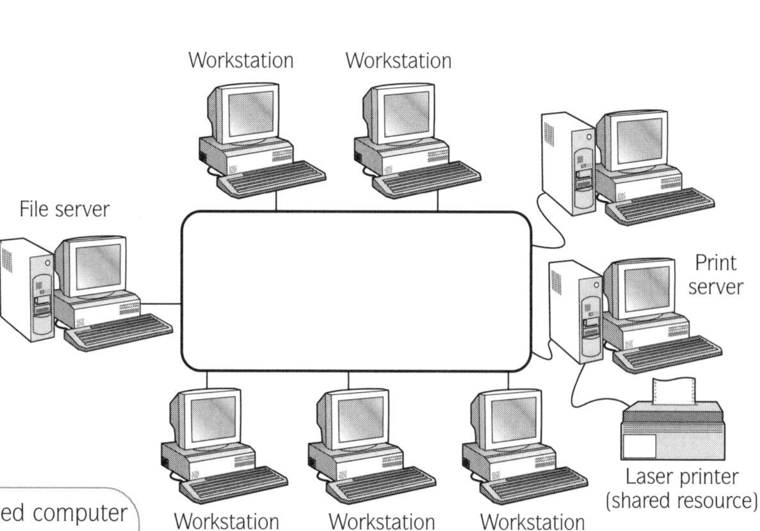

LANs consist of interconnected computer stations within a relatively small area

Fig 1.1

The benefits of using LANs

- LANs are used to share data, which could be in word processing, spreadsheet or database files.
- LANs are used to share peripheral devices such as printers, plotters, scanners and digital cameras.
- You can use a LAN to communicate using e-mail.

Now you try

1. Draw a basic diagram of the network you use in school. Show the printers and other peripherals, as well as the desktops connected to the network.
2. Explain how you would use your school's LAN to share a data file with another member of your class.

Next steps

Network interface cards

What do you need to connect your computer to a LAN? An **interface card** is a device that connects a computer to a network. It stores data coming and going between your workstation and the network, changing it where necessary so that it is compatible with the network.

If necessary the card will convert the data to make sure that it follows the communications rules that run on the network. It may even change the voltage levels of the signals going between your computer and the network.

A network interface card will be fitted to each device attached to the network, whether it be a computer, a peripheral or a server.

Now you try

1. Why is a network interface card necessary?
2. If you attempted to connect your worksation to a network without a network card, what would happen?

Client/server setup

A very common way of organising a LAN is to have a 'client/server' setup. A *client* is a user on a workstation connected to the network. A *server* is a powerful computer which controls a resource that can be made available to a client workstation.

A LAN might have an applications server, a database server, and a web server controlling access to the Internet. All LANs have dedicated printer servers.

Next steps continued

A key part of the network manager's job is to control which network resources a user can access by assigning them *access rights* – for example to specific files on the database server or to specific applications.
When a user logs on to the network, using ID and password, the system checks a user data file which contains IDs, passwords, and details of users' access rights. It then knows whether the user is authorised and, if so, what resources on the network the person is entitled to access.

Wide-area networks (WANs)

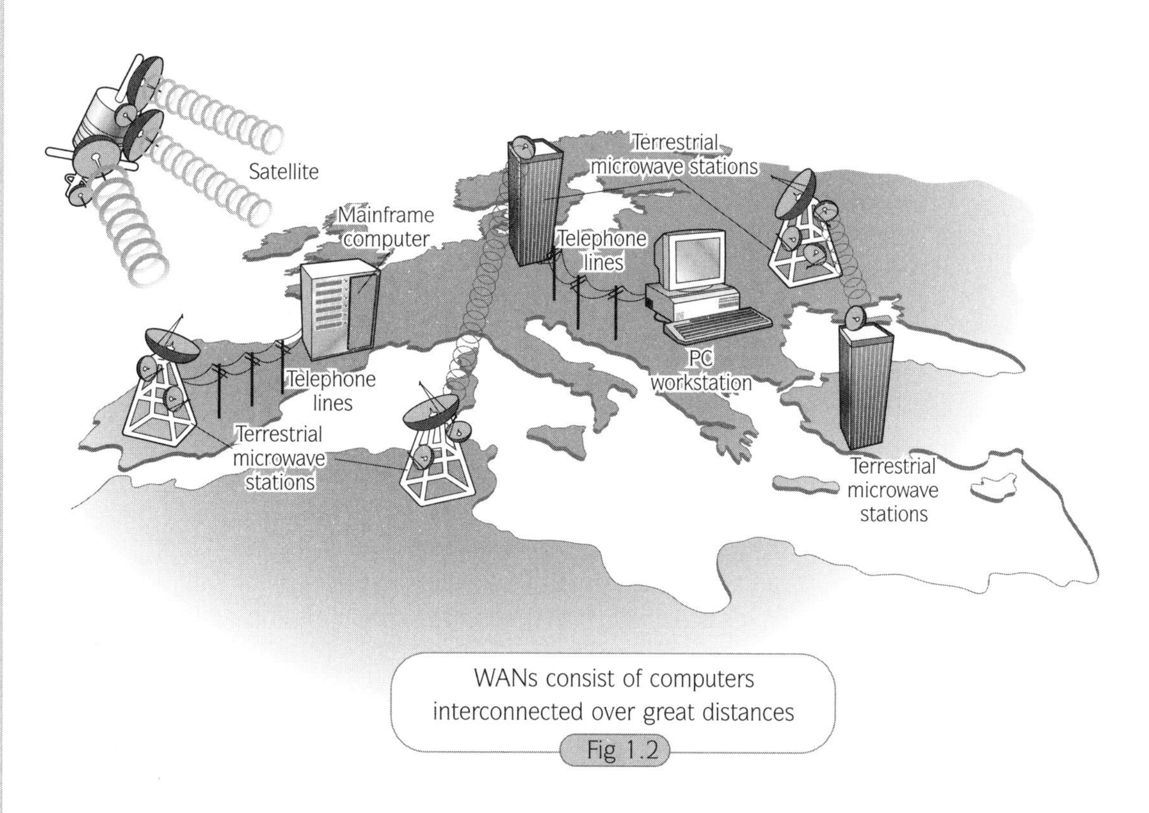

WANs consist of computers interconnected over great distances

Fig 1.2

Wide-area networks link computers across large distances – between towns and countries, right round the world (Figure 1.2). WANs use **telecommunications links** to achieve this.

For example, WANs use telephones and satellites to link the computers, and they use modems. Modems change the computers' digital information into signals that can be sent down phone lines (Figure 1.3). Other modems then change it back again at the receiving end.

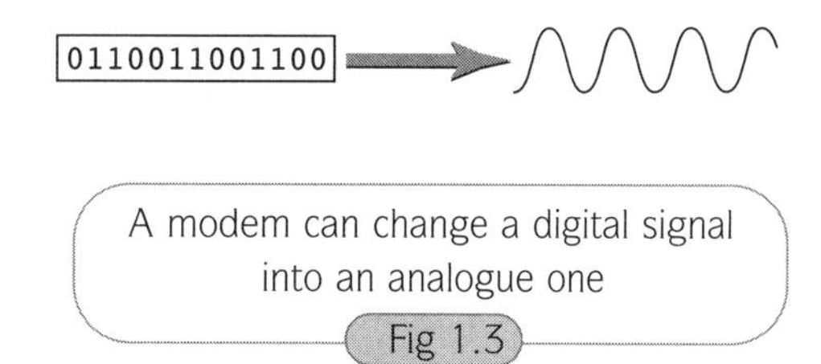

A modem can change a digital signal into an analogue one

Fig 1.3

The benefits of using WANs

Wide-area networks allow people and businesses to communicate over great distances across countries, continents and the world. They are used:

- by businesses – for example to transfer money, to send and receive orders
- to buy and sell things – e-commerce (see page 139)
- to collect information – for example to research a project
- to communicate by e-mail (see page 5)
- to enable people to work together across large distances – for example using video-conferencing (see page 15), or by working from home and linking into the network in the office using a phone connection.

Wide-area networks help people access up-to-date information for their work and leisure and help businesses to compete and survive.

Now you try

1 What kind of modem does your computer have?
2 How fast can it send data down the phone line?

Transmission media

Computer networks use a range of different **media** to transmit their data. The main types of media are copper cabling and fibre-optic cabling.

Copper cabling

Copper cabling generally comes in two main forms:

- *Coaxial cabling*: This is very resistant to interference and is used in networks in industries where there might be a lot of interference.
- *Twisted-pair cabling*: This is the main kind of cabling used in most local-area networks today. It can support transmission speeds of at least 100Mbits per second. It is quite cheap. One disadvantage is that it is not as secure as fibre-optic cabling.

Fibre-optic cabling

Fibre-optic cabling is used in LANs in organisations such as university campuses and for long-distance telecommunications. It works by sending light pulses along fine strands of glass.

Its advantages are that it is secure, free from interference, and transmits at high speeds. However, it is expensive.

Wireless networking

This transmits data through the air using radio waves and microwave frequency radiation. Its advantages are fast transmission speeds and no need for cabling. However, security can be a problem.

Data security

All data files must be protected against corruption, loss or hacking. Let us look at some of the measures that can be taken to protect the data.

System security measures

- *IDs and passwords*: All users are given identity codes and passwords. These make it difficult to access files without proper authority.

- *Advanced ID measures*: Smartcards can be used to store fingerprint or voiceprint information.
- *Data encryption*: This means putting data into a code so that if anyone without authority accesses the data it will be meaningless without the key to the code.
- *Making backups*: Copies of all data must be made on a regular basis and stored in a secure location. A good backup system guarantees that all data can be recovered in the event of files being corrupted or deleted.

Other security measures

- Fit each computer terminal with a lock and key.
- Limit access to rooms with computer terminals, using security locks.
- Use terminals without floppy or CD drives, to make it more difficult for viruses to be transferred.

Knowledge check 1

1. Local-area networks are limited to one building or site. True or false?
2. List *three* benefits of using a LAN.
3. List *three* benefits of using a WAN.
4. Describe a problem that can affect the data link on a WAN.

Credit questions

5. How does a network manager control access to the network's resources?
6. What is the job of a server?
7. What is a client?
8. What is the job of a NIC card?

E-mail

One of the most common ways in which networks are used to communicate is by e-mail. E-mail uses networks to send mail to people. You can send e-mail across a LAN or a WAN, or even across the Internet. All you need, apart from the hardware to connect to your network (see page 7), is to have an e-mail account with its own unique address.

Benefits of e-mail

- You can retrieve e-mail wherever and whenever you want. To read your mail all you have to do is connect with the right network and then sign in using an ID and a password. Figure 1.4 shows a typical e-mail application.
- You can send copies of your mail to several people at once.
- An e-mail gets to where its going very quickly. The time taken is measured in seconds or minutes, depending on whether the item is going across a LAN or around the world via the Internet.
- E-mails are cheap to send. Many Web-based e-mail services are supported by advertising revenue and are free to use.

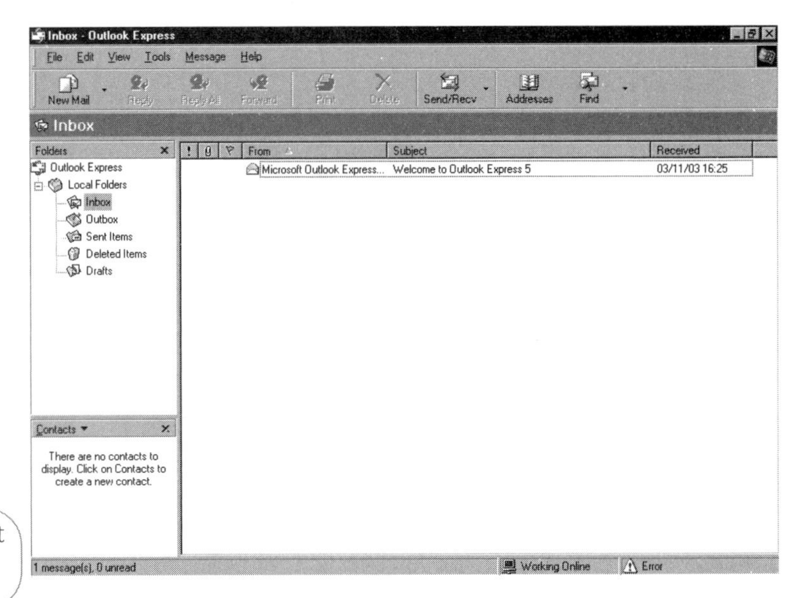

Your computer screen can alert you that a new message has been received

Fig 1.4

Disadvantages of e-mail

- Multiple copies of documents can sometimes arrive, cluttering up your incoming messages box (inbox).
- Files attached to e-mail messages can have viruses hidden in them that can potentially do serious harm to your computer. This possibility can be greatly reduced with suitable precautions.
- When advertisers discover your e-mail address they can use it to send promotional messages. This can be annoying when the messages become frequent.

Next steps

Using e-mail to transfer files across the Internet

An easy way to send files to people is to attach them to your e-mail messages. All you have to do is select Attach file (or whatever your software requires), and then point to the file you want attached. Your e-mail provider then sends the file along with your message. Using this means, you can send text files very quickly right across the world.

Most e-mail providers place a limit on the size of the files that you can send. You should check this before sending a file.

Text messaging

Text messaging is used for messages that are no longer than a few hundred characters. SMS (the Short Message Service) supports messages up to 160 characters long. These are stored at SMS centres and then forwarded to a communication device such as a mobile phone, a palmtop with a phone connection, or a pager.

A similar technology is *instant messaging* (IM) which allows you to send text messages to one or more people on their PC, simply by logging on to the messaging server. Some IM services like MSN even allow you to talk to others in your IM group, provided you have a sound card, a microphone and loudspeakers.

Netiquette

When you use networks to communicate with people by sending e-mails or text messages, you need to keep to a set of rules of conduct known as **netiquette**.

Netiquette is a code which sets out rules of good behaviour and manners which you should stick to when sending text messages, e-mails and postings to e-groups. These rules encourage behaviour that does not upset or inconvenience other people.

The Internet

The Internet is a worldwide system. It uses telecommunications systems to link your computer to other computers and networks right around the world, making it possible for people to share information and communicate with each other (Figure 1.5).

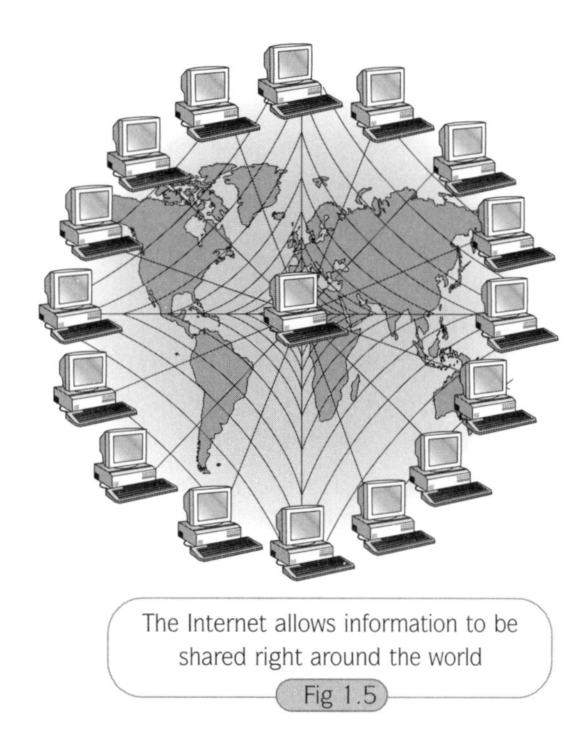

The Internet allows information to be shared right around the world

Fig 1.5

Connecting to the Internet

To connect to the Internet you need to have an **Internet-ready computer**. All you then have to do is plug it in and off you go!

An Internet-ready computer is a normal desktop computer (see page 120), but it is fitted with a **modem** that translates your computer's signals into a form that can be sent down the phone line. It also has **browser** software.

A browser is a program that helps you find your way around the World Wide Web. It finds Web pages for you and then displays them on your monitor. A browser lets you move around from page to page by entering the address of the page or by clicking on a link (Figure 1.6).

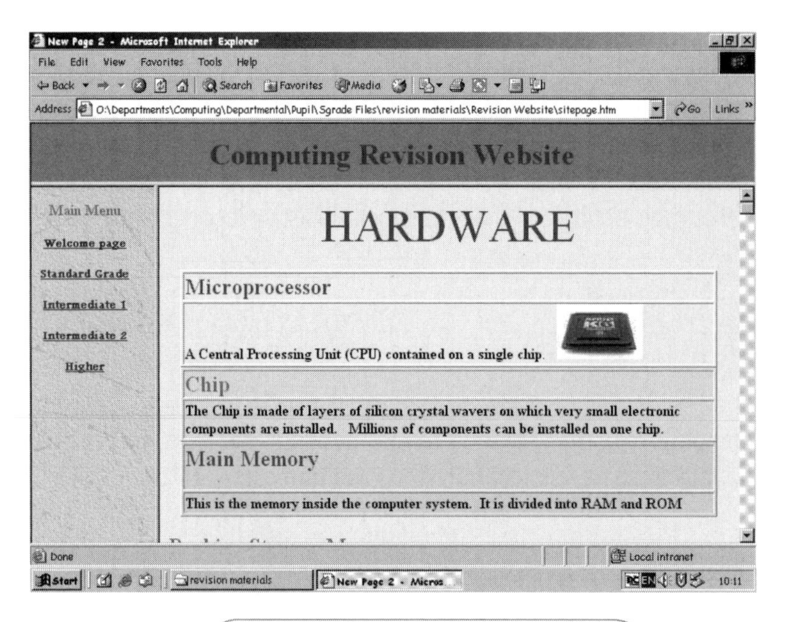

A Web page can be loaded into your browser by using links or by typing the page's address in the address box

Fig 1.6

Telecoms link

You need a telecommunications connection to gain access to the Internet. There are two types of connection you need to know about: dial-up and broadband.

Dial-up access

A dial-up connection uses an ordinary phone line and a modem to connect you to the Internet. Dial-up modems work at a speed of 56Kbits per second (Kbps).

Broadband access

Once you have used a broadband connection you won't want to go back to a dial-up connection. A broadband connection gives much faster access to the Internet.

There are various ways of getting a broadband connection. Two examples are digital subscriber line (DSL) and cable modem.

Look at this table to compare broadband and dial-up speeds:

Connection	*Data transfer speed*
Dial-up line with 56Kbps modem	Maximum of 56Kbits per second
Broadband DSL	Maximum of 512Kbps download and 128Kbps upload
Broadband cable	Maximum of 10Mbps in theory In practice, around 1Mbps is possible because the bandwidth has to be shared with other local users

Next steps

Mobile Internet technology

If you are on the move, instead of using a desktop computer you might use an Internet-ready palm pilot (Figure 1.7). This is an example of a mobile Internet technology. Devices like this are sometimes called 'smartphones' and are a cross between a palmtop and a mobile phone.

A palm pilot
Fig 1.7

Palm pilots can have the following features:

- a touchscreen
- a WIMP interface
- a calendar
- a simple database for contact information
- a calculator
- a browser for Internet access
- a phone which you can use to access the Internet as well as to talk to your friends or send text messages
- a camera to capture images which can then be sent through the network and a video playback facility.

Palm pilots are based on **wireless networking**. That means they use radio waves to communicate data between computers and to access the Internet.

Now you try

Search the Web for information on the latest handheld mobile Internet technologies. Write up a short report on one of them. Include a graphic and as much technical detail as you can find.

Next steps

Internet service providers (ISPs)

Apart from all the right hardware and software, in order to access the Internet you need to have a contract with an ISP. The ISP provides powerful computers called *servers* which you have to log on to to access the Internet. Your computer dials the ISP server and you have to log on using your ID and password.

What your ISP does for you

The ISP server receives, stores and forwards data for your computer. ISPs have servers which give you access to:

- Web pages
- e-mail (see page 5)
- newsgroups
- file transfer sites.

Many ISPs also provide you with:

- free Web storage space where you can store your own pages for other people to look at
- a technical help service in case you run into problems.

Who pays for the ISP?

Most ISPs charge users a monthly fee to cover access and telephone connection. Some others are free to access but involve telephone charges.

Are all ISPs the same?

Internet service providers vary quite a lot according to:

- the costs charged
- the reliability of their system
- the reliability of the connection
- the length of time you can stay connected.

Some ISPs have more powerful computers than others, and this can affect how good their service is.

What you can do using the Internet

The World Wide Web (WWW)

The World Wide Web is made up of linked pages. These pages can contain text, pictures, animated graphics and video clips. There are Web pages of information on any subject you can think of. Your browser can jump between pages easily and display them on your computer. Figure 1.9 is an example.

Hyperlinks

A hyperlink is used to link web pages together. The user clicks on the link to move between one document and another. Hyperlinks are usually either a piece of coloured or underlined text or a graphic.

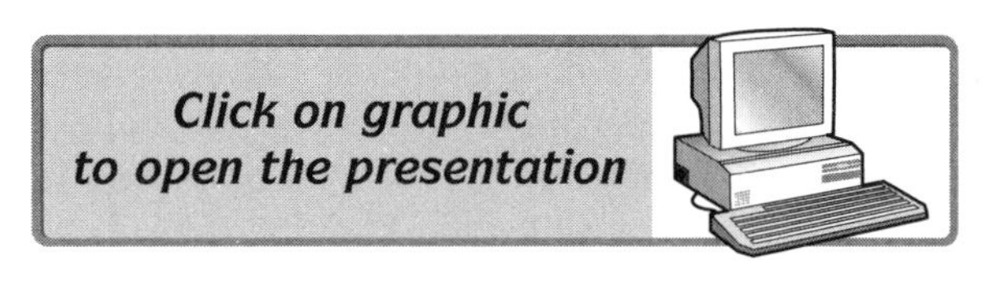

A hyperlink

Fig 1.8

HTML

Web pages are usually put together using an authoring package (see page 61). You can also put Web pages together using a language called HTML, which stands for **h**yper**t**ext **m**arkup **l**anguage. This language uses instructions called **tags** to set up the pages. The instructions or tags are used to describe the colours, graphics, headings and other elements that make up a Web page. Here are a few lines of HTML code:

```
<body bgcolor="#00FFFF">
<p><b><font size="5">Welcome to the Standard Grade Computing
site.</font></b></p>
<p> </p>
<p><b><font size="5">Here you can access help with your
course.</font></b></p>
```

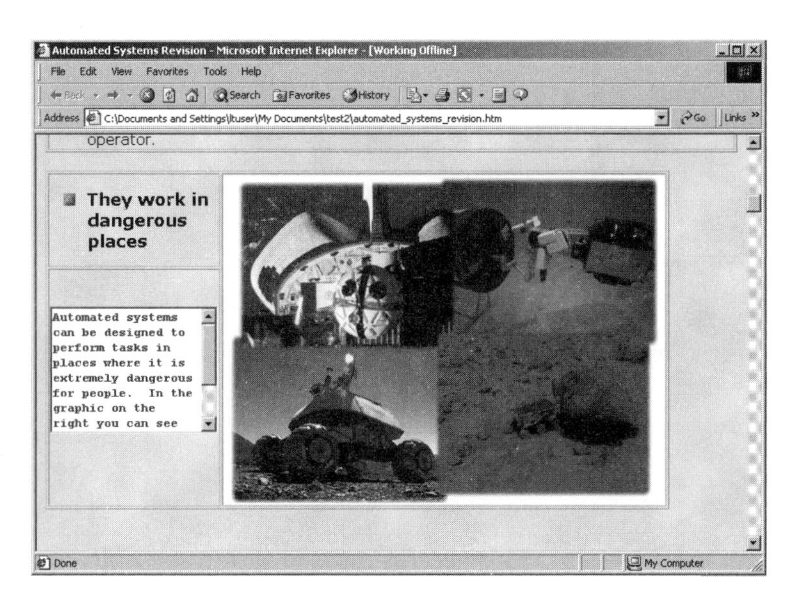

A typical Web page

Fig 1.9

Newsgroups and chatrooms

Newsgroups are subject-based discussion groups. Usenet newsgroups cover many different topics. They are divided into topic areas, such as education, science, the arts, social issues, and leisure. When you join a newsgroup you can join in discussions by posting articles to the group.

Chatrooms are open discussion areas where you can leave messages and have conversations. They are less formal than newsgroups and the discussions can be very wide-ranging. One description of a chatroom is that it is like an electronic school playground.

Search engines

A search engine is actually an on-line database that stores a basic description, and addresses, of lots of Web pages.

Search engines are very easy to use. You simply enter a brief description of what you want to find in the search box and the software does the rest. Once it has done the search it will send the results to your computer and your browser will display the results on your monitor (Figure 1.10).

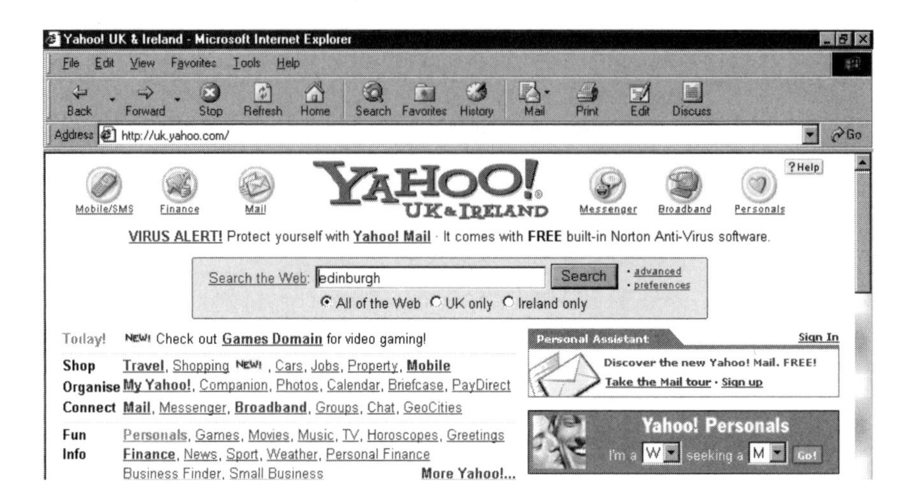

Starting a simple search in a search engine

Fig 1.10

Now you try

1. Write a list of chatrooms and newsgroups you have visited.
2. What is your favourite search engine? Why is it your favourite?

Next steps

Complex searches

If your search criteria are too simple, you can end up with literally thousands of Web pages to check out. This would happen if you were to do a simple search for 'Glasgow'. However, if you entered a more complex search, such as 'Glasgow AND museum OR art gallery NOT transport' you would find links to all of Glasgow's museums and art galleries with the exception of the Transport museum.

Figure 1.11 shows a search engine about to undertake a search for 'castles OR hill forts', but it might be better to add a further key word, such as 'AND Edinburgh'.

Next steps continued

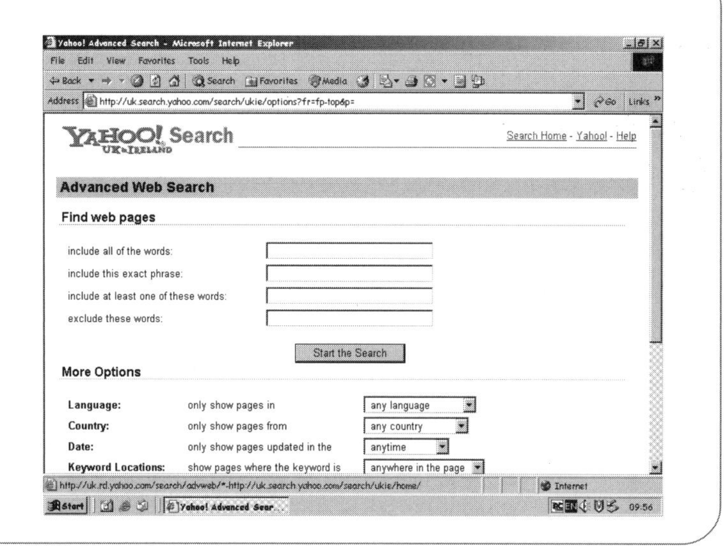

An example of a complex search

Fig 1.11

Buying and selling

Buying and selling on the Internet is known as e-commerce and is dealt with in some detail in the Commercial data processing unit on page 139.

Now you try

1 Describe the services available on the Internet using a table like this:

WWW	
Newsgroups	
Chatrooms	
File transfer	
e-mail	
e-commerce	
Search engines	

Credit questions

2 Write out the complex searches needed to find information on (a) Loch Ness, excluding pages on the 'monster', and (b) tourist accommodation in Edinburgh, to include hotels and guest houses but not bed & breakfast or self-catering.

3 Try out the searches using a suitable search engine.

Knowledge check 2

1 Complete this table:

Advantages of using e-mail	*Disadvantages of using e-mail*

2 What is the Internet?
3 What does a browser do?
4 List *four* services you can access on the Internet.
5 Describe an Internet-ready computer.
6 What is a search engine?
7 What does a hyperlink do?
8 Describe a dial-up connection.

Credit questions

9 What does ISP stand for?
10 What does an ISP do?
11 Give an example of a mobile Internet technology.
12 Give an example of a complex search and explain why you need to have multiple conditions in the search.

Next steps

Software available on the Internet

You might use the Internet to download free software from an FTP site or buy some software from a commercial site. If you do, you ought to be aware of the different types of licences and agreements that are attached to software.

Freeware

You don't have to pay for freeware. It is copyrighted by the author, and usually the conditions of the attached license agreement allow you to use, make and distribute copies of the software but not change it or sell it. Examples of freeware are printer drivers and some games.

Shareware

This is software that comes with a free trial period. After the trial 30 days you have to register and pay a fee. Then you can make copies and give them to other users. They, in turn, then have the same trial period before paying. The reason for selling software like this is that it is a cheap way of distributing and marketing software. There is no need to pay for expensive adverts. The problem is that many people don't register and don't pay.

Commercial software

This is the software you buy from an Internet site. The licence agreement that comes with this software often lays down conditions for your use of the software, such as limiting the copies you can use to one on your desktop and one on your laptop. Making more copies, particularly if you

Next steps continued

sell them, breaks the licence agreement as well as the law (the Computer Designs and Patents Act is discussed on page 71).

Now you try

1 Have you ever downloaded freeware? If so, which site did you go to? What are the conditions attached to the use of the software?
2 If you have never downloaded freeware, do a search and download a useful piece of software and then read the attached conditions.
3 For some commercial software you have purchased, read the main conditions of the licence carefully. You might find a printed copy of the licence, or it may be a document stored on your installation CD-ROM.

Video-conferencing

Video-conferencing can be used to conduct a meeting or conference between two or more people in different places using a computer network to transmit video images and audio signals. A video-conferencing system can be set up on a LAN, a WAN, or even the Internet.

A point-to-point conference

Fig 1.12

Next steps continued

A *point-to-point conference* is a simple setup with two people each sitting in front of a computer screen. The computer system is equipped with a video camera, a microphone and a set of speakers (Figure 1.12). The camera and microphone are used to input the sounds and images which are then transmitted over the network to appear on the monitor of the other person. The network will have to be able to transmit at a fast rate, in order to cope with the amount of data involved.

A more complex setup is known as *multi-point conferencing*. Here the network is used to link people from three or more distant locations using a WAN. For example, Edinburgh, Paris and New York could be linked in a virtual conferencing room.

The advantages of multi-point conferencing for a business are:

- it saves the time and expense of getting people to one location
- it can quickly bring together experts to solve problems, no matter where in the world they are located (Figure 1.13).

Video-conferencing can involve many people in discussions

Fig 1.13

Multi-access computers

Businesses have 'mainframe' computers that allow many people to use them at the same time. But how do they work?

Multi-access computers share the main processor by giving each user a slice of the processor's time (Figure 1.14). Each time-slice is a tiny fraction of a second. The process goes round the users so fast that they don't realise they are sharing the processor with perhaps hundreds of other users (see the Computer systems unit, page 121).

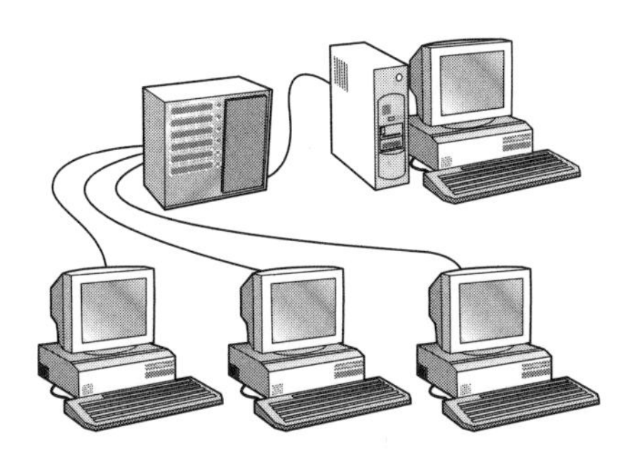

Multi-access computers share a main processor

Fig 1.14

Social, legal and ethical issues

Social issues

Information rich/poor

This issue is all about access to the wealth of information that is available to us on networks. You can use the Internet to gather information about any subject – perhaps a subject you are studying at school, about jobs, banking and finance, entertainment, and home shopping.
If you have ready access to this information it gives you a head start in whatever you are doing. But some people don't have access to this information and so can be at a disadvantage.

Social inclusion

The problem is about how to include everyone in the network-based 'information age', how to let everyone have the benefits of access to the information out there on computer networks.
This is becoming less of a problem as time goes on. There are more and more ways of accessing network-based information: at school, at work, at home, in libraries, in Internet cafés, even through a mobile phone.

Social isolation

Some people don't mix with other people very much and prefer to spend their time on the Internet playing games, checking out websites and sending e-mails. This can be a lot of fun, but some people can become isolated and lose out on meeting other people.

Legal issues

Breaking copyright

Networks make it easy to transfer files around the world. This provides people with many opportunities to break the law by transferring music files, software or other copyrighted materials without paying a fee.

Next steps continued

Hacking

Some people use networks to hack into computer systems and place viruses, or copy or delete information. Some people even hack into bank networks and steal money from accounts.

Invading peoples' right to privacy

Networks can be used to invade people's privacy by accessing personal data or sending junk mail.

Ethical issues

Using networks to spread distasteful materials

Unfortunately one of the problems with networks is that, in the wrong hands, they are an efficient way of spreading distasteful materials – e.g. of a violent or a sexual nature. Some people even use networks to spread racism, sectarianism or other forms of hatred.

Using networks to spread chain letters or nuisance letters

There are people who think it is fun to spread abusive mail using the Internet. In fact this causes distress in a lot of people.

Networks are very powerful communication tools. They should be used responsibly to educate, to inform and to allow people to communicate with each other. There are codes of behaviour which set out how we should behave when using networks: see netiquette on page 7.

Knowledge check 3

1. How does freeware differ from shareware?
2. How many copies of a commercial software package are you normally allowed to make?
3. Where on the Internet are you likely to find (a) freeware, and (b) shareware.
4. What is the difference between multi-point and point-to-point video-conferencing?
5. Why do businesses use video-conferencing?
6. What is a multi-access system?
7. Describe how networks can be used to break laws on copyright and privacy.
8. How can people who have no access to the information held on networks be disadvantaged?

End of unit progress check

Questions

1 Imagine you work for an insurance company. The offices are spread across several floors of a high-rise office block. Describe two advantages for the company of having a LAN. 2

2 What types of network (a) connect computers in one building, and (b) connect computers across countries and continents? 2

3 List *three* ways in which Ford Motors would benefit from having a WAN. 3

4 Complete the table:

This changes the computer's digital information so that it can be sent down the telephone line	
This means your computer is connected to a network and ready to send and receive data	
This is a language for defining Web pages	

3

5 What software does your computer have to use to help you find your way around the World Wide Web? 1

6 'All you can do on the Internet is to look at Web pages': true or false? Give *three* examples to support your answer. 3

7 Your friend is having trouble finding the Web pages she wants to see. What advice could you give her? 1

8 State *three* advantages of using e-mail. 3

9 What does a computer need to make it 'Internet ready'? 2

Foundation/general total 20 marks

Credit questions

10 How could you access the Internet while on a train journey? 1

11 Why do you need a network interface card in order to plug a computer into a LAN? 3

12 A client/server network is set up in your office. You are asked to give a simple explanation to the staff about how it works. What would you say? 2

13 You search the Web for pages on castles. You get thousands of suggested links. How can you cut down the number of pages your search turns up? Give an example. 2

14 'I have to choose an ISP. I don't know where to begin. There are loads of them to choose from.' What advice would you give? 3

15 'Shareware and freeware are the same thing. Anyway, I can do what I like with any software I download from the Net.' Why is this statement neither accurate nor very clever? 2

16 Scotware, an international software development company, has multiple projects on the go at any one time. It has experts working for it in many countries. Suggest ways in which it can use video-conferencing to make its business more successful. 2

Credit total 15 marks

General-purpose packages

What you will read about in this unit

- General-purpose packages and why we use them
- Storing data in general-purpose packages
- The human–computer interface
- Software integration
- Common features of general-purpose packages
- Features of word processing applications
- Features of spreadsheet applications
- Features of database applications
- Features of graphics applications
- Desktop publishing
- Presentation and multimedia
- Web page creation
- Expert systems
- Jobs, money, security and the law

General-purpose packages and why we use them

General-purpose packages are software packages that are designed to let you, the user, carry out a wide range of tasks. The packages you must know about for the Standard Grade Computing course are word processing, graphics, spreadsheets, databases, presentations and multimedia. Some examples are shown in Figure 2.1.

Some general-purpose packages

Fig 2.1

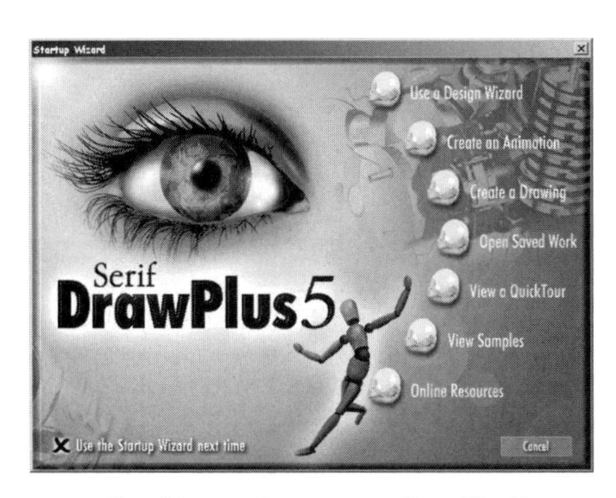

Graphics packages, e.g. DrawPlus5

Word processing packages, e.g. Word:mac

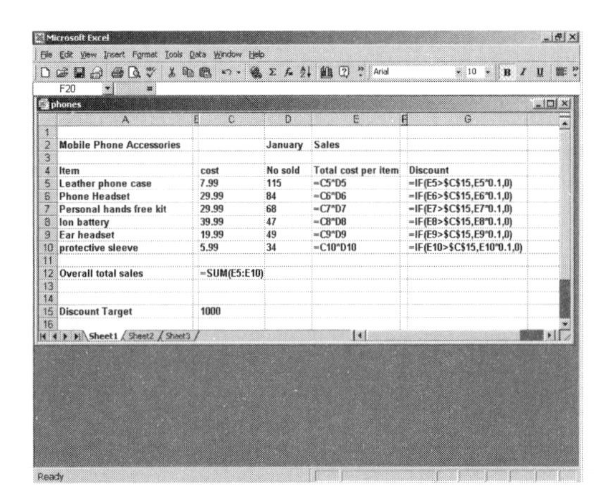

Spreadsheet packages, e.g. MS Excel

Database packages, e.g. FileMaker Pro7

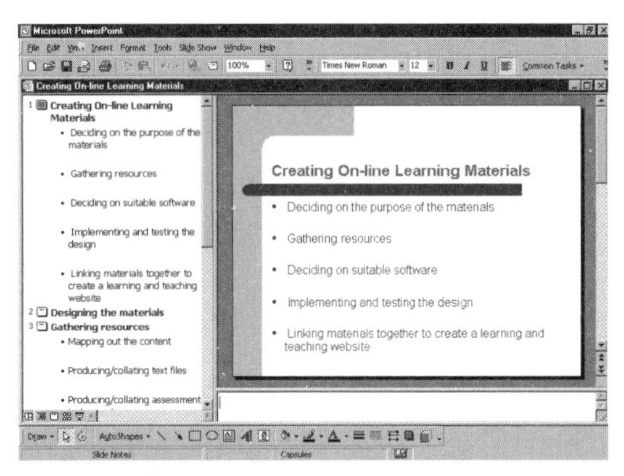

Presentation and multimedia pacakges, e.g. MS PowerPoint

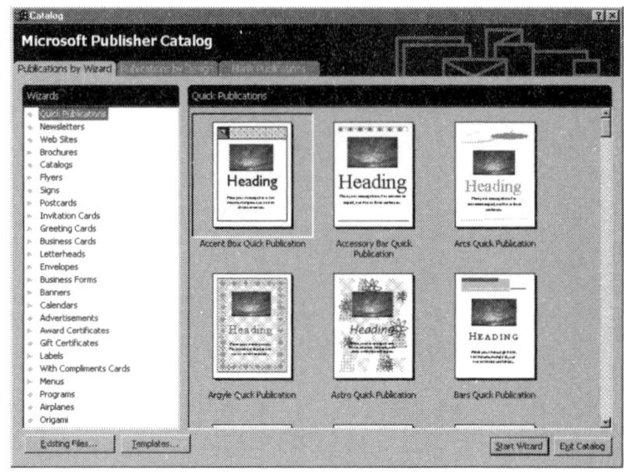

Desktop publishing packages, e.g. MS Publisher

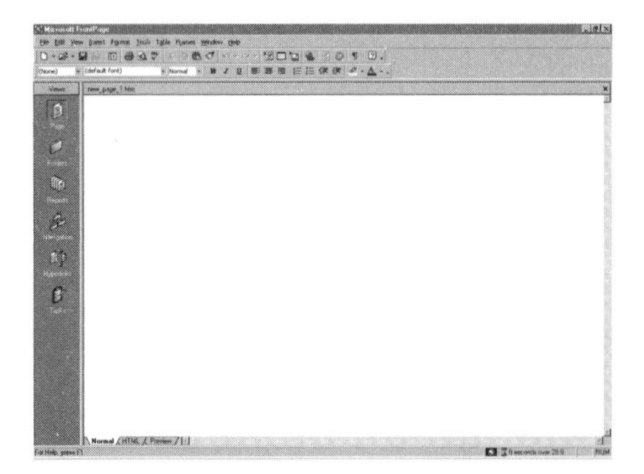

Web page creation packages, e.g. MS FrontPage

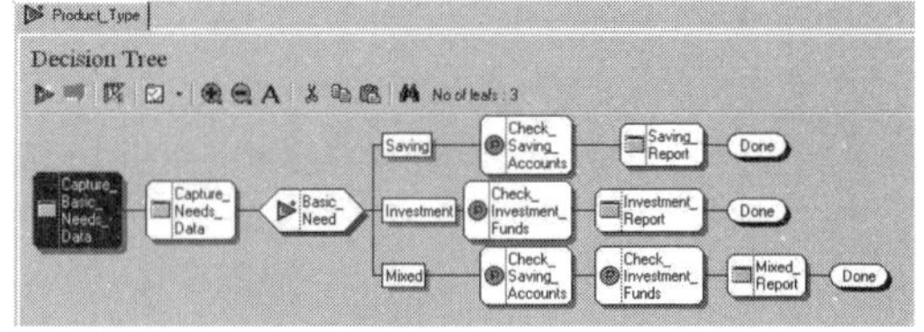

Expert system packages, e.g. XpertRule Knowledge Builder

General-purpose packages increase your ability to carry out tasks efficiently in various ways.

- *They save time.* The time taken to search for information, to update and get printed copies is reduced.
- They help to ensure your *data does not get lost* – provided of course that you take care to save data properly and to make backups (see page 27).

- They help you keep your information *accurate and up to date,* if you take care when entering it into the system.
- You can use them to *communicate* by creating documents and sending them to other people using computer networks.
- They can *help reduce costs* in the long term, though they can be expensive to buy.
- They allow you to be *flexible* in the way you produce documents. You can easily change the content, style or layout of a document at any time.

Now you try

1. Write down the general-purpose packages you are going to use on this course.
2. Write a short paragraph outlining the reasons for using general-purpose packages.

Storing data in general-purpose packages

Numbers, text and graphics

Numbers

The package designed to handle numbers is a **spreadsheet**. This lets you store numbers and carry out complicated arithmetic using formulae (see page 44). An example is shown in Figure 2.2.

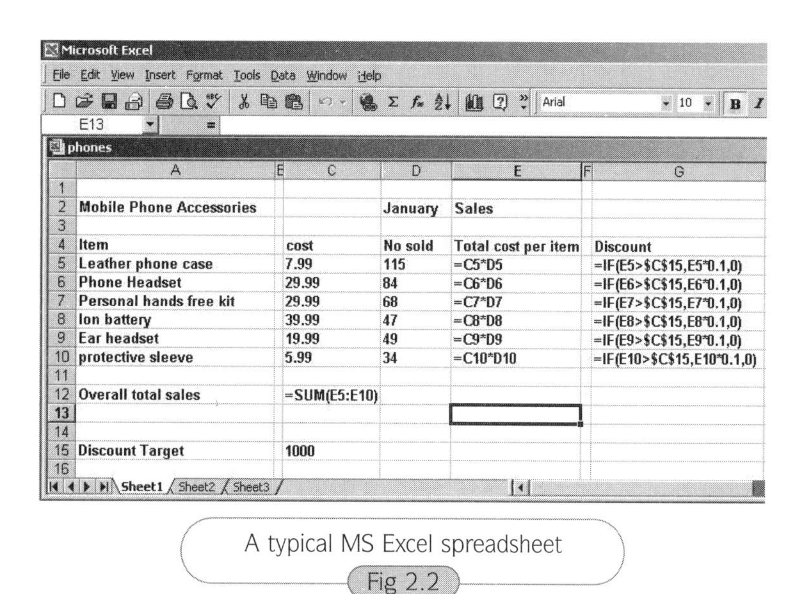

Microsoft Excel

File Edit View Insert Format Tools Data Window Help

E13 =

phones

	A	B	C	D	E	F	G
1							
2	Mobile Phone Accessories			January	Sales		
3							
4	Item		cost	No sold	Total cost per item		Discount
5	Leather phone case		7.99	115	=C5*D5		=IF(E5>C15,E5*0.1,0)
6	Phone Headset		29.99	84	=C6*D6		=IF(E6>C15,E6*0.1,0)
7	Personal hands free kit		29.99	68	=C7*D7		=IF(E7>C15,E7*0.1,0)
8	Ion battery		39.99	47	=C8*D8		=IF(E8>C15,E8*0.1,0)
9	Ear headset		19.99	49	=C9*D9		=IF(E9>C15,E9*0.1,0)
10	protective sleeve		5.99	34	=C10*D10		=IF(E10>C15,E10*0.1,0)
11							
12	Overall total sales		=SUM(E5:E10)				
13							
14							
15	Discount Target		1000				
16							

Sheet1 Sheet2 Sheet3

A typical MS Excel spreadsheet

Fig 2.2

Numerical data can be stored in other general-purpose packages. For example, word processing packages number the pages of documents, databases can store numbers as well as text, and graphics packages can use numbers to label drawings and illustrations.

There is more information about spreadsheets on page 44 and more on storing numbers on page 104.

Text

The package designed to handle text is a **word processor**, of which there is an example in Figure 2.3.

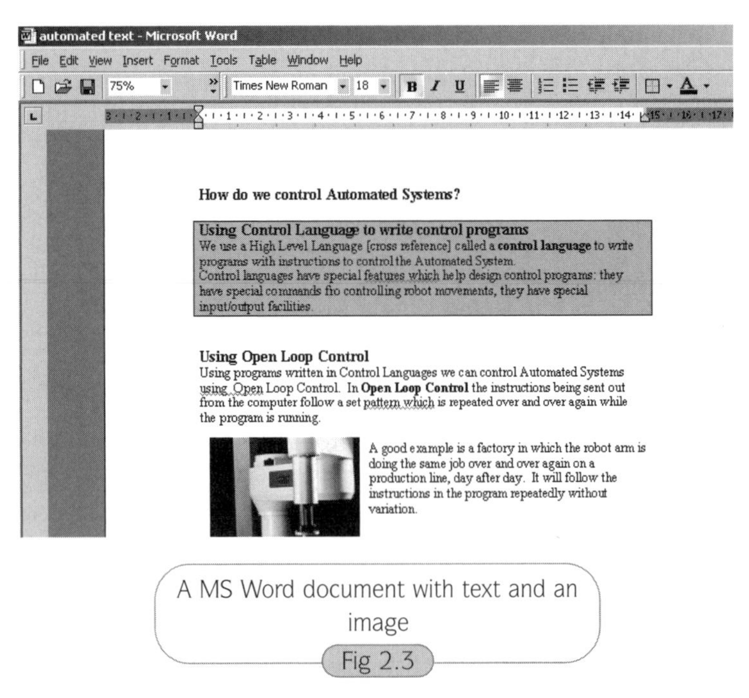

A MS Word document with text and an image

Fig 2.3

You can use your other packages to store text. Databases can store text items like names and addresses, and spreadsheets and graphics packages use text to label columns of figures and drawings.

You can take a closer look at word processing in the section beginning on page 40, and there is more information on storing text on page 105.

Graphics

The package designed to handle graphics is, obviously, a **graphics package**, of which there is an example in Figure 2.4.

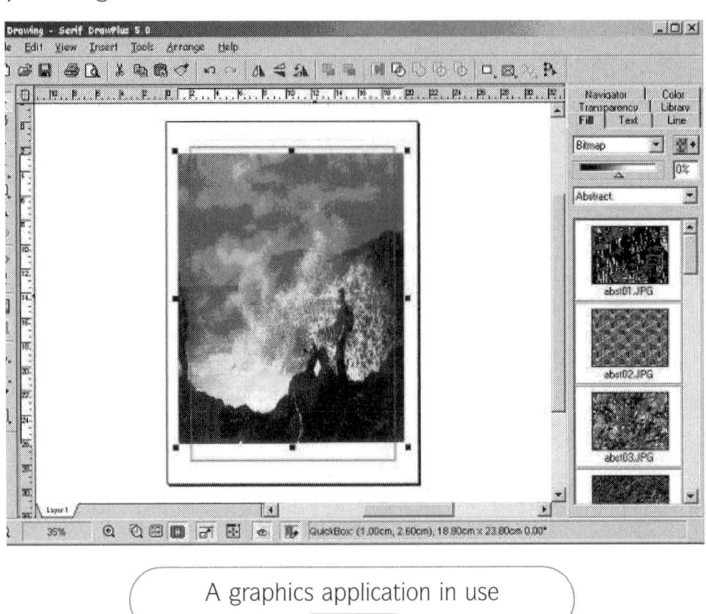

A graphics application in use

Fig 2.4

You can, of course, find graphics in the other packages: word processing, spreadsheet and database packages can all contain graphics.

Find out more about graphics packages on page 54 and about graphic data on page 105.

Now you try

Print a screenshot of a document, containing numbers, text and graphics, from each of your packages.

Audio and photographic data

Audio and photographic data includes multimedia packages, such as web creation packages, that deal with sound files and the graphics files produced by digital cameras.

Audio data

Many software packages can handle audio data. Audio data can be stored and processed in two distinct ways: as MIDI and as digital audio.

- A MIDI audio file actually stores the instructions needed by the system to create a sound. For example, it will have information about the pitch and length of a note.
- A digital audio file stores a digital representation of the sound, which it obtains by taking samples of the sound wave. Details of exactly how this is done is covered in the Computer Systems unit when we look at audio cards (see page 121).

One problem with digital audio files is that they can be very large and therefore place heavy demands on the computer's memory and backing storage. Storing data in digital audio WAV format, you can store just 70 minutes of music on a 700 megabyte writable CD. It is preferable to compress the data to make the file size smaller. For example, using the compressed MP3 file format you can store 700 minutes of music on a 700 megabyte writable CD.

Photographic data

When you take a picture with a digital camera, the camera stores a digital representation of the image in its memory. You can then transfer this digital image to your computer and process it using a range of graphics software. Exactly how this is done is covered in the Computer systems unit (see page 115).

A problem with graphics images is that the files can be very large indeed, and – like audio files – they are often compressed before being stored and used.

The photograph in Figure 2.5 has been saved as an uncompressed bitmap (BMP) file and as a compressed jpeg (JPEG) file. The bitmap is 404 kilobytes in size and the jpeg file is 34 kilobytes . . . quite a difference!

A huge saving in file size can be achieved with compression

Fig 2.5

Next steps

Animations

GIF animation is a common way of creating animated (moving) graphics. To create the animated effect the software displays a series of still images one after the other. In animation software each still image is called a *frame*. To get a good realistic level of animation the system has to process around 24 frames per second.

The computer has to store a binary number for each pixel on the screen and repeat this for every frame in the animation. This can take up a lot of processor time and means the files can be very large.

If you want to speed up your animations, you can use Shockwave or Flash. These produce much smaller animation files which take up less disk space and are more suitable for use in Web pages.

Video images

Video file sizes can be very large indeed. If you are recording at a speed of 30 frames per second and one colour frame requires 1 megabyte, then the camera will have to store 30 megabytes per second, or 1800 megabytes per minute. There is more information on digital video on pages 115–116. It is obvious that there is a need to compress the video images, otherwise it would be very difficult to store and process them with current technology. Most video images are now compressed into MPEG-2 files, so that they become less than one-fiftieth of the original size. They can then be stored on a DVD and processed.

Now you try

1. If you have any animated graphic files on your system, list them and examine their file sizes.
2. Why do animated GIFs demand so much space?
3. Describe how animated GIFs work.
4. Pick your favourite movie. How long did it last? How much space would it take on your hard drive or DVD?
5. Why are most video files stored as MPEG-2 files?

Making backups

After entering any data into a computer it is wise to make a **backup** copy. A backup is an exact copy of your data that you can resort to if the original is lost for some reason. Computers can break down, disks can develop faults, and you can delete things by mistake. So you need to make backups on floppy disks, hard disks, tapes or writable CDs and store them in a safe place.

Next steps

File formats

You can save text documents in various file formats. The most common are ASCII, plain text and RTF (rich text format).

The advantage of using these *standard* formats is that they are recognised by a wide range of applications. This means that you can transfer text from one application to another.

ASCII

A file saved as an ASCII file has all the information about the words, characters and spaces. It has none of the information about the formatting of the document such as the text style, the paragraphing, the indentation.

Because it lacks the formatting information, an ASCII file will be more compact than many other formats. It will thus demand less storage space and be quicker to transmit across a network. For more information about ASCII, see page 105.

Plain text

This format is virtually identical to ASCII. It encodes plain text with no formatting information. However, text format includes the code which allows it to divide text into paragraphs.

Rich text format

A file saved in rich text format (RTF) has all the formatting information which the ASCII file lacks as well as the actual text. It includes all the information about styles, fonts, sizes, paragraphing and indentations.

Knowledge check 1

1. Which general-purpose packages are you going to learn about?
2. Write out *four* reasons for using general-purpose packages.
3. Give examples of where you would find numbers (a) in a spreadsheet, (b) in a word processing document, and (c) in a database.
4. Give examples of where you would find text (a) in a spreadsheet, (b) in a word processing document, and (c) in a graphics file.
5. Briefly describe *two* types of audio data applications have to deal with.
6. How do digital cameras store data about photographs?
7. What are backups and why are they necessary?

Credit questions

8. Describe (a) how animated GIFs work, and (b) a disadvantage of animated GIFs.
9. Why do we need to compress video data?
10. What are the advantages of saving a file in (a) ASCII and (b) RTF formats?

The human–computer interface

This is the part of the computer that you, the user, interact with. You use the human–computer interface to give the computer instructions to do things like load files and start or close an application. It is called the **HCI** for short.

The types of HCI you need to know about are:

- the WIMP (windows, icons, menu, pointer)
- the GUI (graphical user interface).

Graphical user interfaces

The most common way to control a computer is to use a **g**raphical **u**ser **i**nterface, or GUI for short. With this type of interface you use a range of on-screen graphics to control the computer – such as clicking on an icon, ticking boxes, or selecting a value using spin boxes (Figure 2.6).

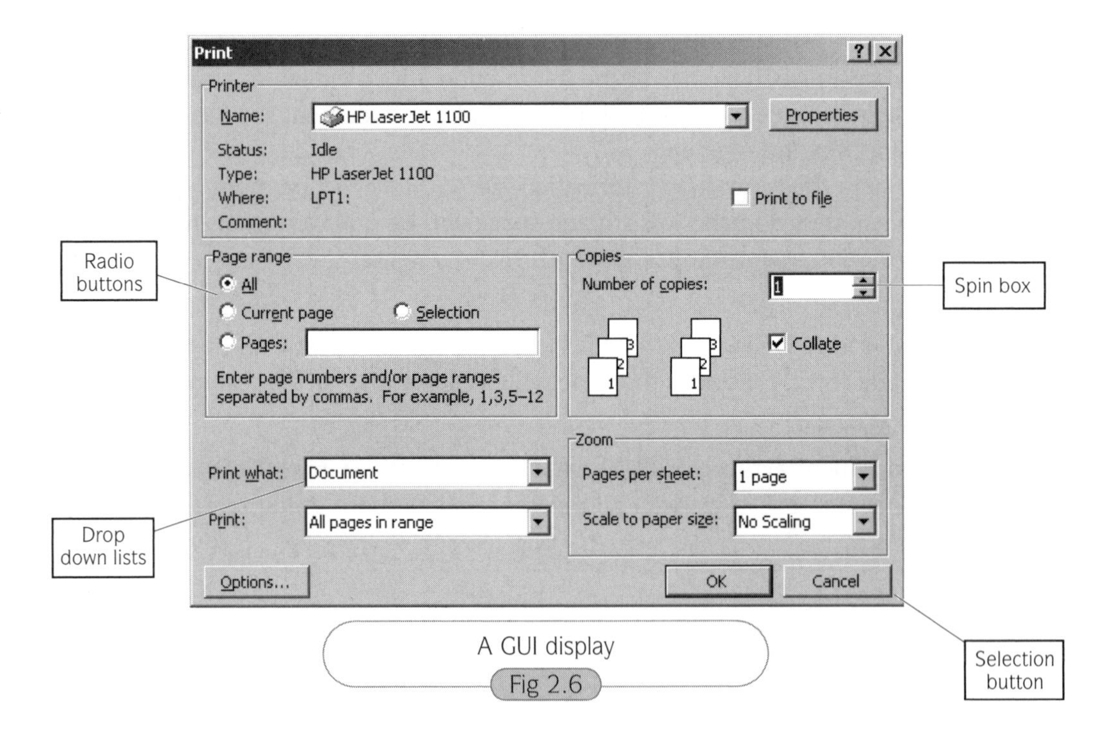

A GUI display
Fig 2.6

Toolbars

A toolbar is a type of menu which offers the user a series of icons to get things done. Figure 2.7 shows a drawing toolbar. Note that the drawing icons are all gathered together to make the user's task easier.

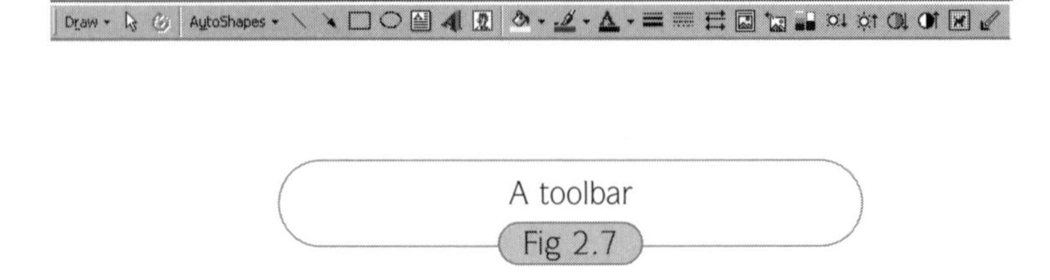

A toolbar
Fig 2.7

The WIMP environment

Another common type of interface is known as WIMP, which is short for 'windows, icons, menu, pointer'.

A window can, for example, display what is in a folder or a document (Figure 2.8). Icons represent items such as software, files, folders, hard disks, printers or scanners (Figure 2.9). Menus give you choices from which you can make a selection (Figure 2.10). You use the *pointer* and *mouse* buttons to select icons and items on menus.

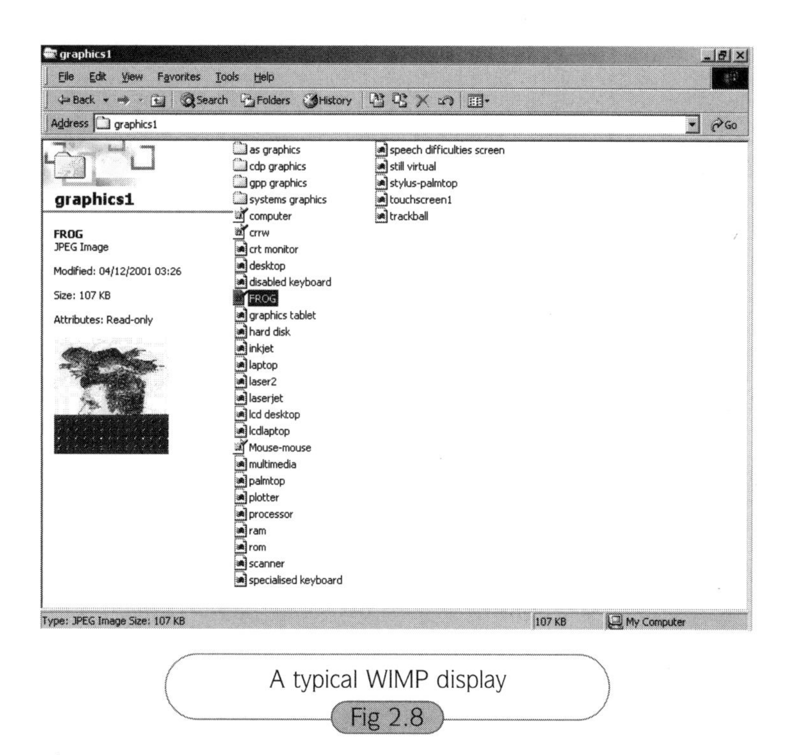

A typical WIMP display

Fig 2.8

A WIMP human–computer interface is very '**user-friendly**'. That means that it is very easy to use. With some practice and a little help you can quickly learn how to work with the software. To control the computer all you have to do is select icons and items from menus using the pointer, and open and close windows. What could be easier?

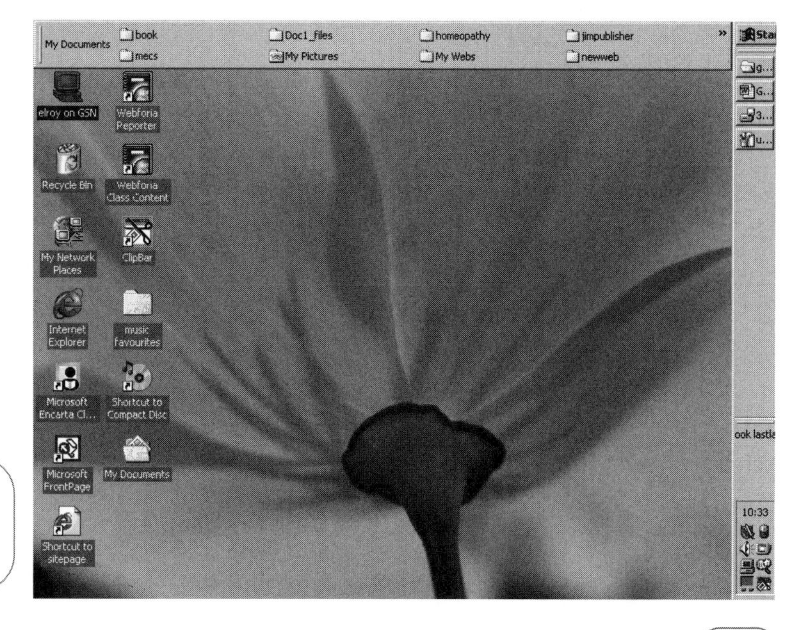

Icons represent items such as software, files, folders, hard disks, printers and scanners

Fig 2.9

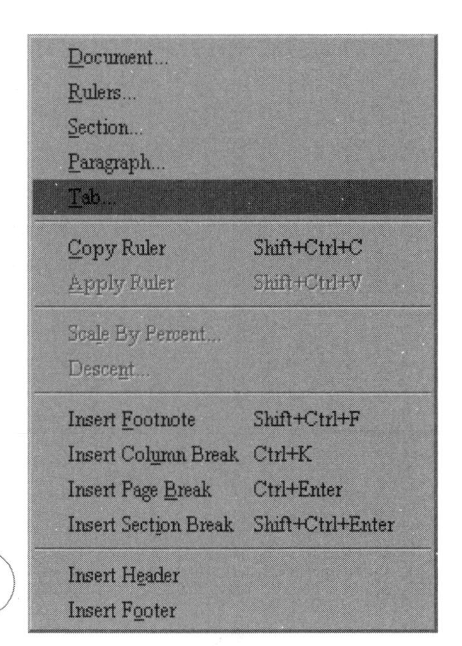

A typical menu display

Fig 2.10

Now you try

1. List *six* of the icons on your desktop.
2. Open the window of your *My Documents* folder. What does this show you?
3. Use your pointer to open a few documents and select a few items on the Edit menu.
4. Open an application and find a toolbar. Experiment with it. Find out what it can let you do.
5. Why is a toolbar a useful part of your HCI?

Getting help

If you get stuck when using your database package, say, where do you get help? At school you could ask your teacher, but alternatively most general-purpose packages have their own help files. All you have to do is select **Help** and then type in what your problem is. Your computer will then attempt to find the help file you need and display it for you. An example is shown in Figure 2.11.

Some packages even have an **on-line tutorial**. This explains how to operate a package and takes you through examples. It then sets you exercises so that you can practise your skills. An example is shown in Figure 2.12.

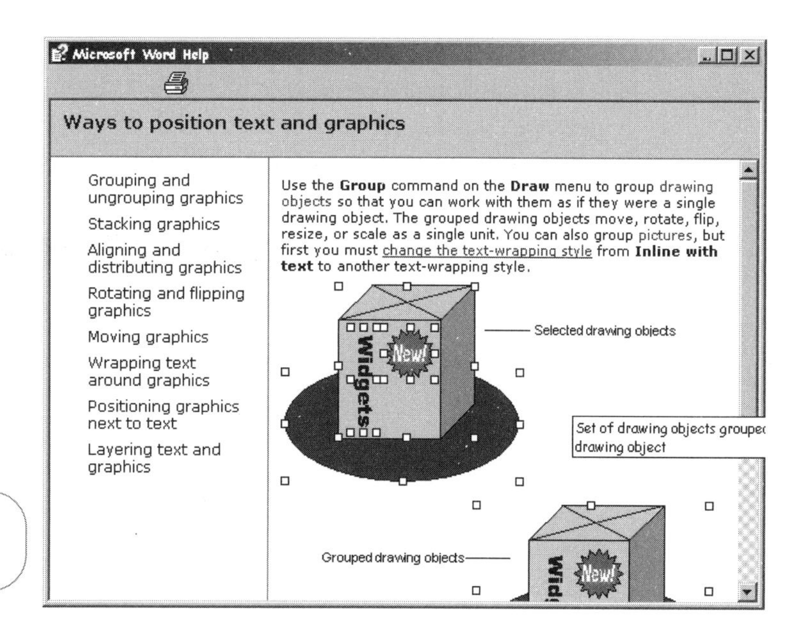

Help files are intended to answer frequently asked questions

Fig 2.11

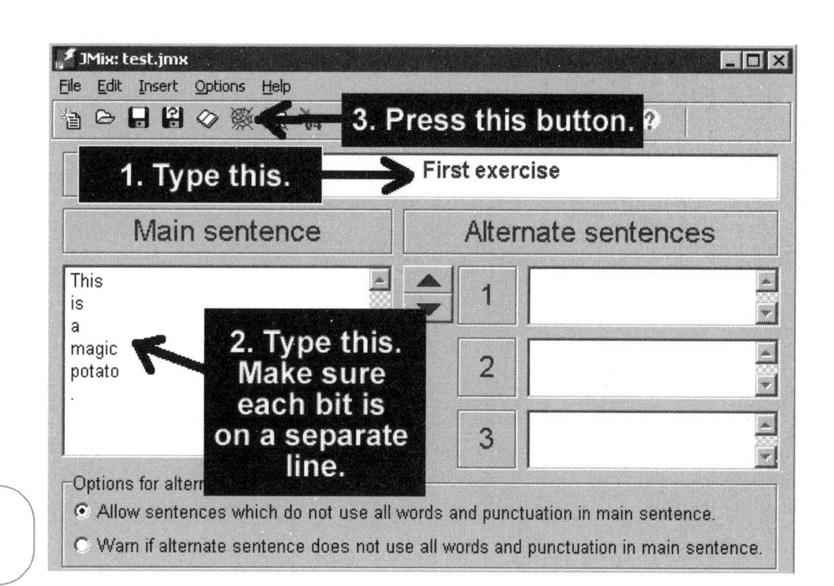

On-line tutorials are another way of learning how to use software

Fig 2.12

Now you try

1. Experiment with the on-line help in your word processing package. Ask it how to use search and replace, and how to insert a graphic.
2. If you have an on-line tutorial available for one of your packages, open it and have a go at some of the exercises.

Templates

Many applications come with templates to help the user set up documents. Templates are *outline* documents with key features of the document structure already set up – such as font sizes and frames for headings and main text boxes (Figure 2.13).

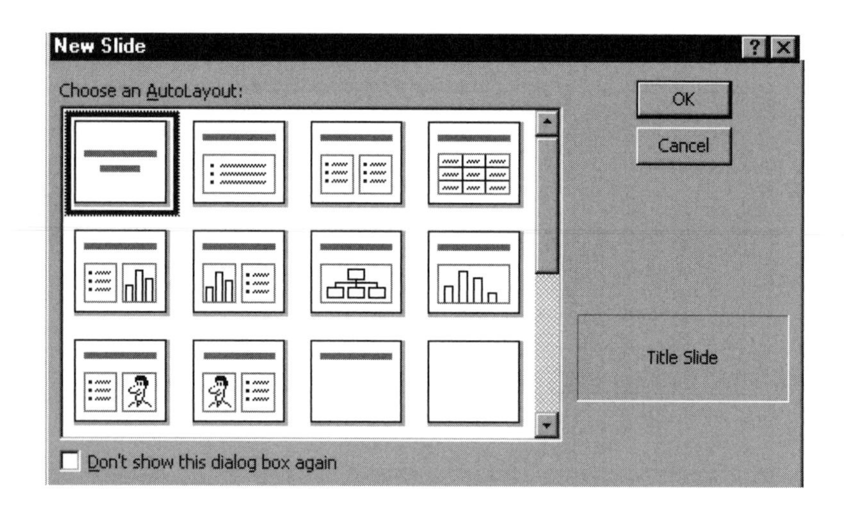

Templates get you off to a good start

Fig 2.13

Now you try

1. What advantages are there in using a template?
2. You can find templates in virtually all your applications. Open up one of your applications and set up a simple document using a template.

Wizards

A wizard is a piece of software that guides you step by step through a complicated process – such as installing some software, setting up a template or creating a document. You can find wizards in most applications.

The wizard uses a series of dialogue boxes and screens to step you through the process. Figure 2.14 shows two of the dialogue boxes the Microsoft Excel wizard uses to help you to create a chart.

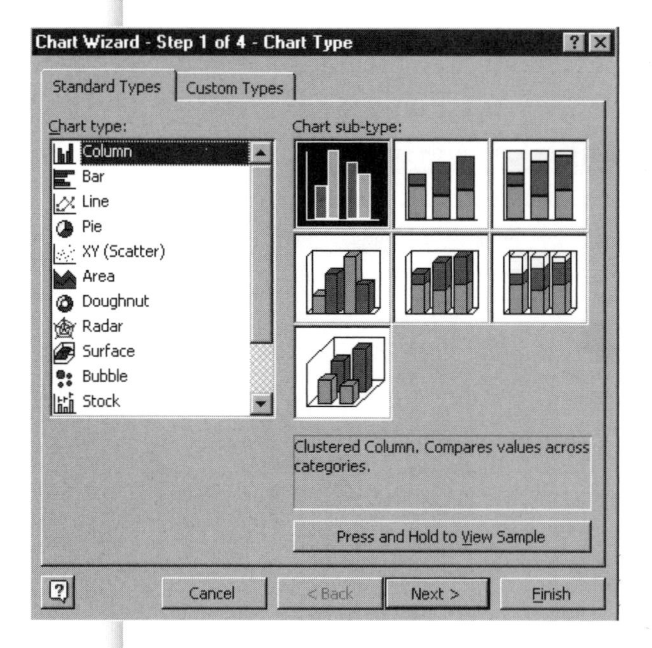

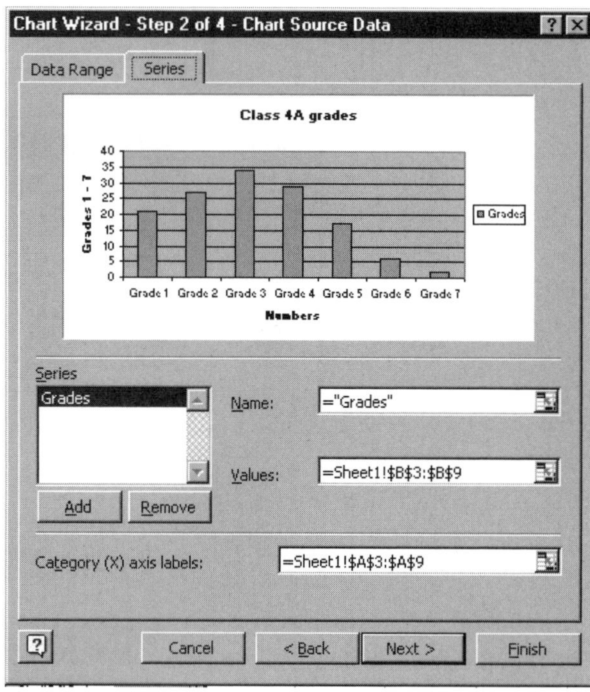

Wizards take you along step by step

Fig 2.14

Now you try

Locate and use a wizard that is available in one of your general-purpose packages. Write up a short report on your use of the wizard. You should illustrate your report with screenshots.

Next steps

Customising your HCI

This sounds complicated, but all it means is that you can change some parts of the HCI to suit yourself. You could change the size of the icons, the background colour of your desktop, or the speed of movement of the pointer. Most computers let you do this by using a **control panel** (see Figure 2.15).

Keyboard shortcuts

Sometimes it is quicker to press a key (or a combination of keys) to get things done, rather than go through a series of menus. A good example is shown on the menu in Figure 2.16, which lets the user *copy and paste* using the control (**Ctrl**) key and letter C to copy (to the Clipboard), and then **Ctrl** and the letter V to paste, without the need to bring up the menu at all. It is a good idea to memorise the shortcuts you find you are using most often.

Next steps continued

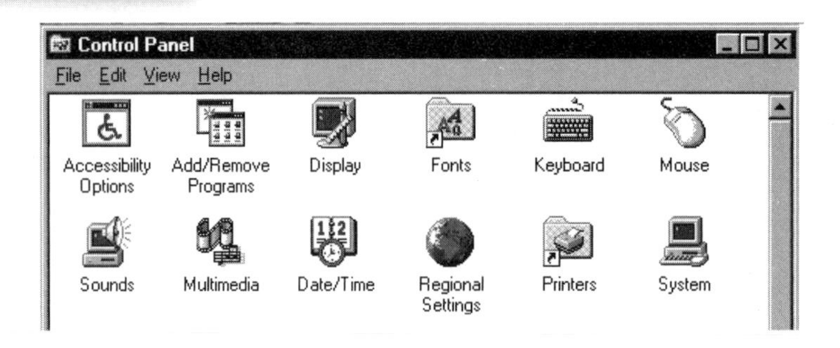

A control panel
Fig 2.15

Keyboard shortcuts
Fig 2.16

Now you try

1 Try customising your desktop. Change the background colour and the size of your icons. Open a directory/folder and show all the details of your files, then arrange them alphabetically.
2 Open up a word-processed document and cut and paste a couple of paragraphs using the keyboard shortcuts.

Knowledge check 2

1. What does HCI stand for?
2. What does WIMP stand for?
3. What makes a WIMP so user friendly?
4. What is an icon?
5. What are icons used to represent?
6. How would you describe on-line help?
7. In what way is an on-line tutorial (a) similar to on-line help, and (b) different from on-line help?
8. Describe how a template you have used helped you produce a document.
9. Describe how a wizard would help you set up and label a graph.
10. What is a toolbar?

Credit questions

11. Describe *two* ways in which you have customised your HCI.
12. Why are keyboard shortcuts useful?

Software integration

An **integrated package** combines several applications in the one package. An example is AppleWorks (Figure 2.17). Most integrated packages have the following applications:

- word processing
- spreadsheet
- database
- graphics.

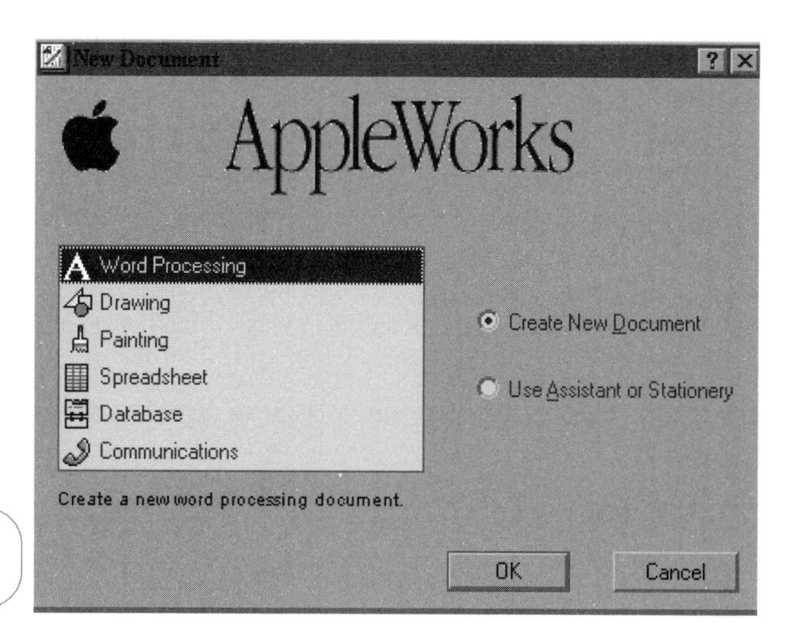

AppleWorks is an example of an integrated package

Fig 2.17

There are several benefits to this type of integration:

- the applications have a common HCI
- transferring data between the applications is made easy
- you can set up dynamic links between files.

The common HCI

All the applications have a common human-computer interface. This means they have similar icons, menus and commands. Figure 2.18 shows three Edit menus from an integrated package – notice how similar they are.

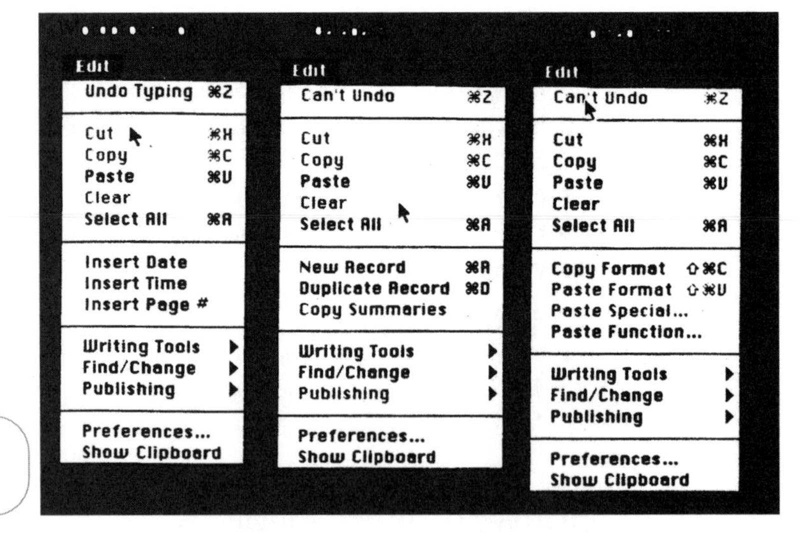

Menus in integrated packages have a uniform look

Fig 2.18

This makes learning to use an application a lot easier. Once you are familiar with the menus and icons in, say, the spreadsheet then you will find using the word processor quite straightforward.

Ease of data transfer

If you use an integrated package you can easily transfer data from one application to another. It's as easy as copying and pasting. Whenever you have to produce a document where you need to combine data from different applications, an integrated package is ideal.

A report prepared by the sales manager in a car showroom might combine data from the following applications:

- a written report on sales – from the word processor
- sales figures – from the spreadsheet
- information about employees – from the database
- illustrations and diagrams – from the graphics application.

This is just the sort of job for an integrated package. Look at the report in Figure 2.19: it uses the integrated package to combine data from the graphics and spreadsheet packages.

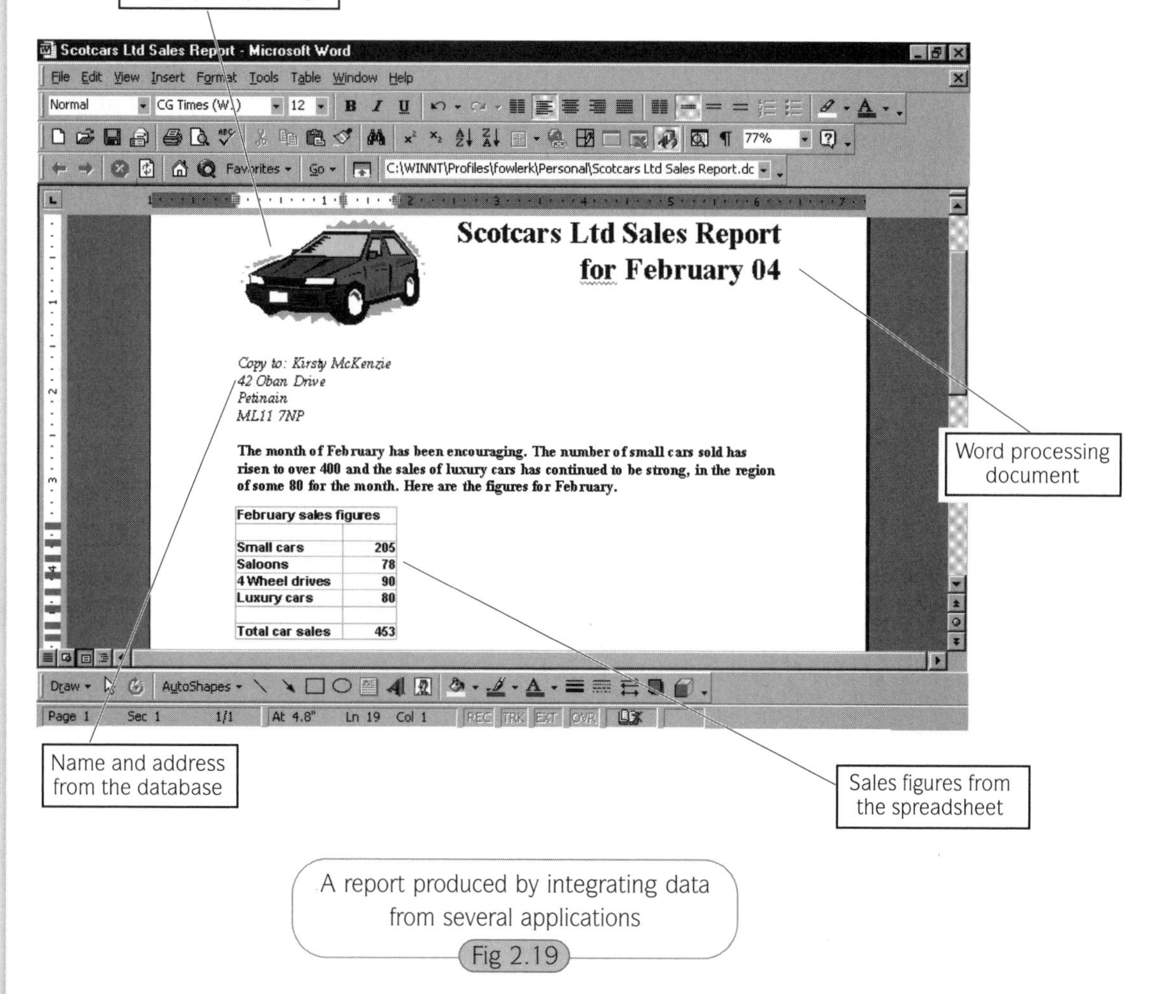

A report produced by integrating data from several applications

Fig 2.19

Now you try

1 Decide which integrated package you are going to use and write down the name.
2 Open up a word processing document and look carefully at the Edit menu. Now open up the Edit menus in the spreadsheet and database applications. You should find that they are very similar, because they have a common HCI.
3 If you have data files for each type of application, try copying data from the spreadsheet and pasting it into the word processing document. Transferring data between applications in an integrated package is quite easy to do.

Next steps

Links between files

Dynamic links

Integrated packages let you set up dynamic links between files so that when you change data in the source file, the data in the linked file is updated automatically.

In the sales report in Figure 2.19, the number of monthly car sales could be linked to a spreadsheet file. If the total in the spreadsheet is changed, the report will be automatically updated, without the user having to do anything. The advantage is that the software is making the update for you. One less thing to remember!

Static links

You can also set up static links between files. This means that you can insert objects from one file into another. However, unlike dynamic links, if you change the source file the linked file does not change – you have to select it directly and make any necessary updates.

Now you try

1. Set up a word processing document and a spreadsheet with a few numbers and a simple formula to add up the numbers. You may need to read pages 40–47 as well as seeking help from your teacher and/or the on-line help in using these packages.
2. Now set up a dynamic link between your spreadsheet file and your word processing file.
3. Prove to yourself that it works by changing the spreadsheet data. The linked data in the word processing document should update automatically.
4. Now set up another link, this time a static one. Write down what happens if you change the source data.

Integrated suite of applications

You can also find integration achieved by having a suite of separate applications which, apart from having a common HCI, use common data formats. This means you can transfer data between the applications with ease, often by a simple cut-and-paste operation. Microsoft's MS Tools suite is a classic example of this approach to integration (Figure 2.20).

An advantage of this approach is that each application will have a much wider range of features than those you find in software which integrates all the applications into one package. A disadvantage is that it requires so much more hard disk space and main (RAM) memory.

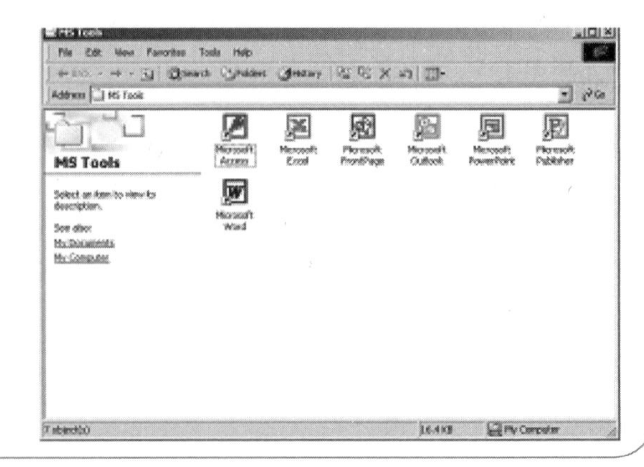

MS Tools is an example of an integrated suite of applications

Fig 2.20

Knowledge check 3

1 What is an integrated package?
2 State *two* advantages of using an integrated package.
3 Why is a common HCI useful in an integrated package?
4 How would an integrated package be used to produce a report on the exam results of your class?

Credit questions

5 Explain how a dynamic link works.
6 What is the advantage of using a dynamic link?
7 What is the difference between a static link and a dynamic link?
8 Describe (a) an advantage and (b) a disadvantage of using an integrated suite of applications.

Common features of general-purpose packages

You need to know about the following applications in detail: *word processing*, *databases*, *spreadsheets* and *graphics*. You will learn about the main features of each application. After that you can try a few practical tasks to make sure you have understood the basic ideas.

First, there are a number of features that all four applications have in common. Some of these are summarised in Table 2.1.

Table 2.1 Features common to all four applications

Feature	*What you need to know*
Open an application	Start the application by selecting an icon or choosing from a menu.
Create, save or print a file	Set up a new file, save it or print it by selecting an icon or choosing from a menu.
Insert data	Use the pointer and keyboard to enter data into a file.
Amend data	Make a change to data.
Delete	Get rid of data from a file using the delete key or delete the whole file using an icon.
Change the appearance of text	Change the style and making it **bold** or *italic*, changing the size, or changing the font.
Move data	Using copy and paste or cut and paste you can move text around a document.
Headers and footers	These are areas at the top and bottom of a document in which you can put things like page numbers, titles and dates that you want to appear on all pages.
Print part of a document	The **Print** options enable you to specify which pages of a document you want to print.

Now you try

1. Open a word processed file you have saved on disk and alter its appearance by changing the font and size.
2. Insert a header and/or a footer into one of your documents. The header could contain the title, and the footer could contain the page number, and perhaps the filename as well.
3. Finally, print the *first two* pages of your document.

Features of word processing applications

Entering text

Text is usually entered at the keyboard, but you can also scan in some text (see page 43) and even use voice recognition. A **spellchecker** can be used to help you find and correct your spelling mistakes. Figure 2.21 shows an example of part of a document.

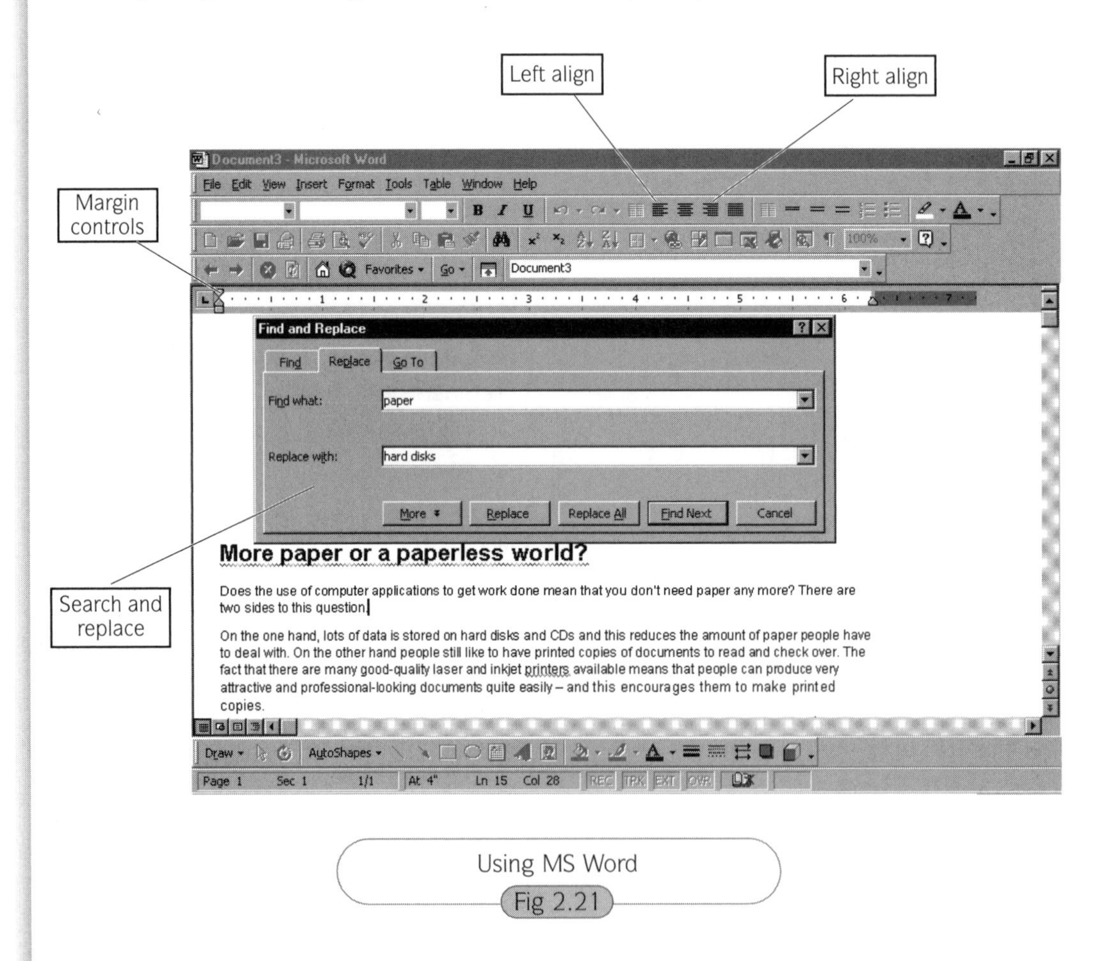

Using MS Word
Fig 2.21

Altering line length and alignment

You can change the length of each line of text by adjusting the **margin markers** at the top of the page. **Wordwrap** automatically moves words on to the next line so that they fit inside the margins. You can change the **alignment** to right-align, left-align or centred by clicking on the alignment icons.

Altering the page length
You can choose from a menu of set page lengths, or set your own. Usually your pages are set by default to A4. Page breaks can be inserted manually if required.

Page layout
You can change the way the text is laid out on the page. You can also change the way headers and footers are set on the page.

Using tabs
You use tabs to set text out in columns by using the tab key.

Search and replace (find and replace)
You can use this to find and change words you have used throughout a document. The function *finds* the word and then automatically *changes* it for you if that is what you choose. This can save a lot of time.

Standard paragraphs
One particular paragraph of text can be used over and over again. You can type it out, store it on disk then call it up and insert it into a document, saving time and effort.

Text style
You can change the appearance of the text by selecting bold, italic or underline.

Check grammar
This feature helps to make sure that your document sticks to the rules of the English language. The feature can usually be switched off.

Tables

A table is an object that helps the user to format (organise) the layout of text entries in a document. It is made up of **rows** and **columns** which the user specifies using a dialogue box (see Figure 2.22).

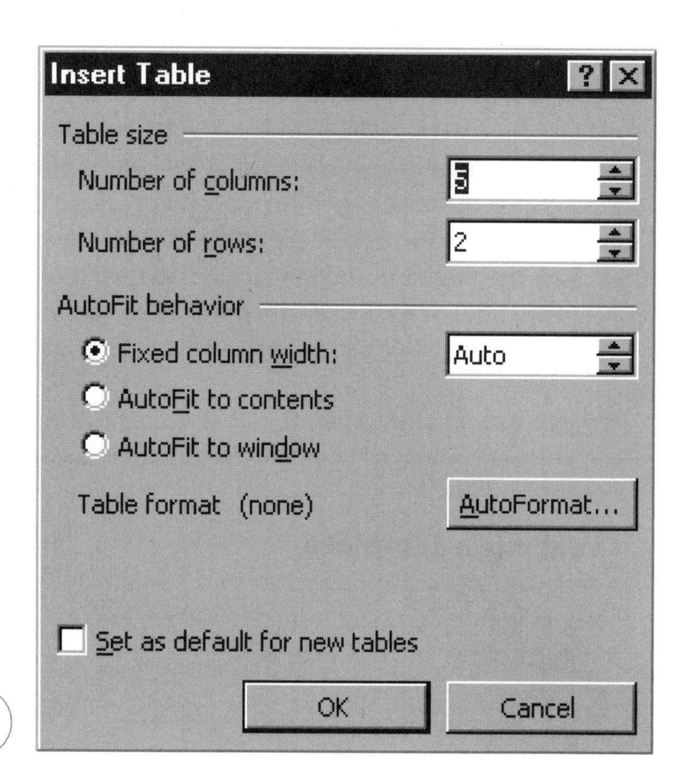

How a new table is set up
Fig 2.22

You can do lots of things with tables. For example, the cells can be set to automatically expand to fit text and graphic entries. You can also add extra columns and rows, and you can merge adjacent rows and cells.

There are many uses for tables in a document, among them:

- organising data into categories
- highlighting comparisons between entries
- controlling the position of text and graphics
- making your web pages look neat.

Now you try

Think how you could use a table when producing the following documents: (a) a personal web page for you and your friends; (b) a report for your English teacher, comparing two short stories; (c) a contact list with all your friends and family on it.

Next steps

Standard letters

A standard letter is one that will be used repeatedly and sent to many different people. It is typed without names and addresses on it. These are then added from a database file as the letters are printed out. This is known as *mail-merging*.

Mail merge

A mail merge operation uses a word processing application *in combination with* a database application to produce, for example, a series of personalised documents quickly and efficiently.

A mail merge is commonly used to produce sets of standard letters. The procedure for setting up a mail merge can be divided up into the following steps.

1. Set up a master document using the word processing application.
2. Indicate the locations in the document where the data which is about to be merged has to go.
3. Save the master document file to the hard disk.
4. Link the master document to a database file containing, say, names and addresses.
5. Instruct the system to begin the mail merge and take the data from the database file, place it into the specified part of the word processing document and print out the required number of copies.

A major benefit of mail merge is that it uses the ability of your computer system – both hardware and software working together – to automate a complex and repetitive task in order to save production time.

Creating a template

A template sets out the structure of a document. It holds all the information about layout, style, headers and footers, and format. Creating a new template is usually a simple matter of following the instructions in a dialogue box.

Next steps continued

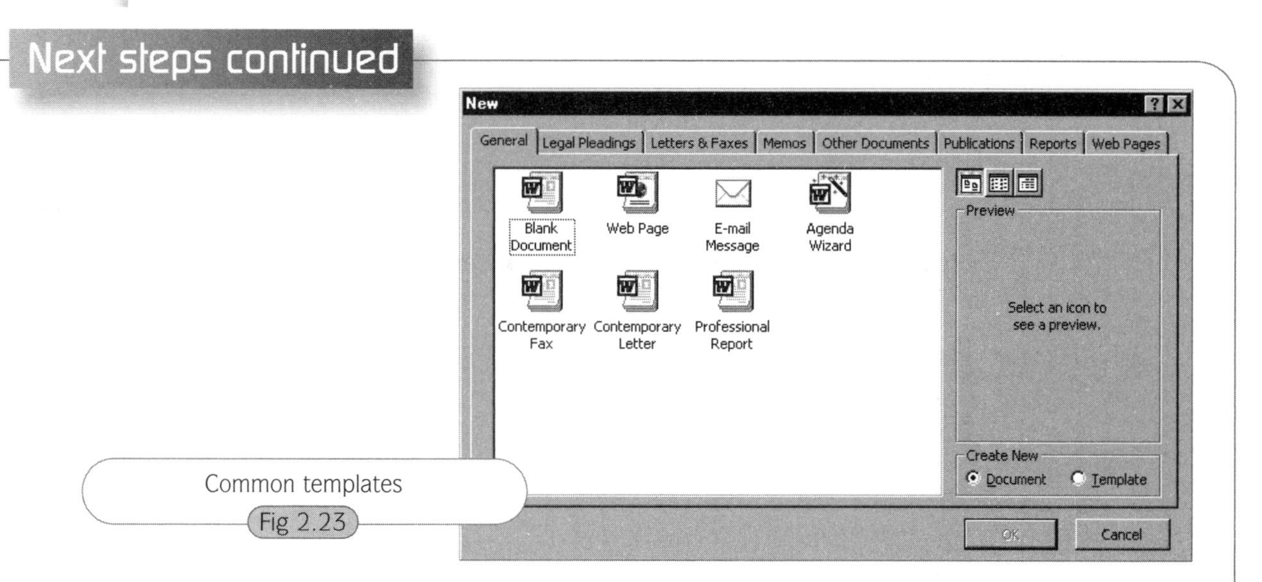

Common templates

Fig 2.23

Now you try

1 Ask your teacher to help you set up a mail merge on your system. If you are working on your own, check out the help files on the word processing application in your integrated package.
2 List the steps involved in setting up a mail merge.
3 Why is a mail merge an efficient way for a business to advertise in order to get more customers?

Optical character recognition (OCR)

Optical character recognition (OCR) software is used to enter text into a computer by means of a scanner. A scanner produces a digital image of a page by reading in the light reflected off the page surface (see page 115). The OCR software interprets the digital data, comparing the shapes of the text with those in its memory. When it finds a match it stores the code for the matched character. In this way text can be quickly entered into the system without the need for time spent at the keyboard.

Once the OCR software has finished interpreting the characters, you can check and edit the text using a word processing application. The main advantage of OCR is that it greatly speeds up data entry, saving the user time and the business money. One disadvantage is that the software is rarely completely successful in recognising the text charaters, so that some time has to be spent checking the accuracy of the scanned text.

Now you try

1 How does an OCR application read in text from a document?
2 You have a paper copy of a 10–page typed report sent to you by surface mail ('snail mail'). You need to amend some parts and add some tables before printing it out again. What is the most efficient way to do this?

Features of spreadsheet applications

Spreadsheets are designed to help you process numbers. They let you store numbers and do arithmetic on them. They are made up of the rows and columns where you place numbers and the formulae you need to do the calculations. Figure 2.24 shows an example.

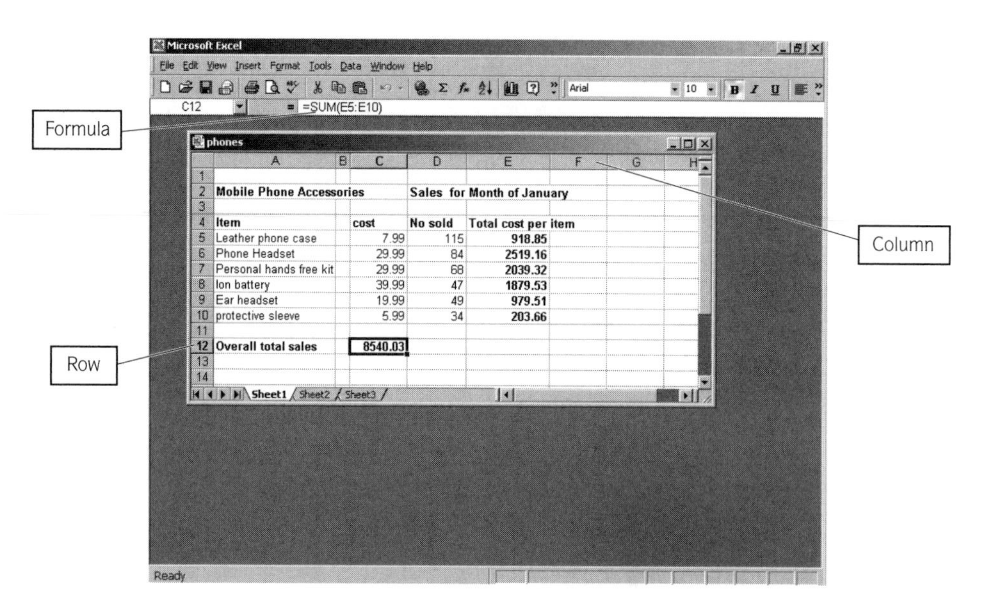

A spreadsheet is basically a table with labelled rows and columns

Fig 2.24

Cells, rows and columns

A spreadsheet is made up of **cells**. A cell is where you store a value. You address a cell by using the column letter and row number (e.g. B4). A **row** is a line of cells which goes from left to right across a spreadsheet; the rows are numbered 1, 2, 3 etc. A **column** is a line of cells which goes from the top to the bottom of a spreadsheet; at the top of each column is a letter, A, B, C etc.

Altering the width of a column

Occasionally you need to make a column wider to make room for more text or numbers.

Altering cell attributes

The attributes of a cell define the **format** of the data the cell will hold and display (Figure 2.25). Examples are dates, currency, time, scientific, fixed to two decimal places.

Entering text

You can enter text, usually as a heading for a column or a row.

Values

A value is usually a number or a formula, but it can sometimes be a string (or combination) of characters.

Formulae

A formula is a definition of the calculation to be carried out on cell contents. You should know these simple formulae:

- =sum(A2..A6)
- =average(B3..B12)

- =MAX(C4:D8) – this calculates the largest value in the range
- =MIN(E3:E10) – this calculates the smallest value in the range

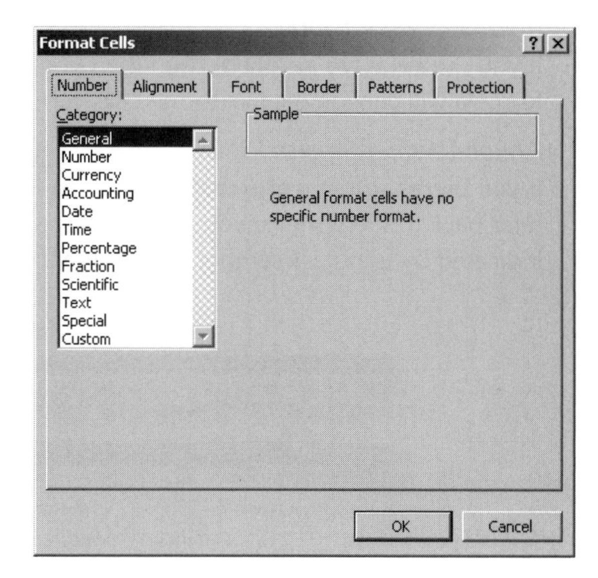

Cell attributes can be altered by the user

Fig 2.25

Inserting extra rows or columns

Sometimes you need to add a row or a column into a spreadsheet to make room for more numbers or formulae.

Replication

To *replicate* a formula is to copy it across a row or down a column.

Charting

You can turn numbers in a spreadsheet into a chart. This makes it easy to see at a glance what they mean (Figure 2.26).

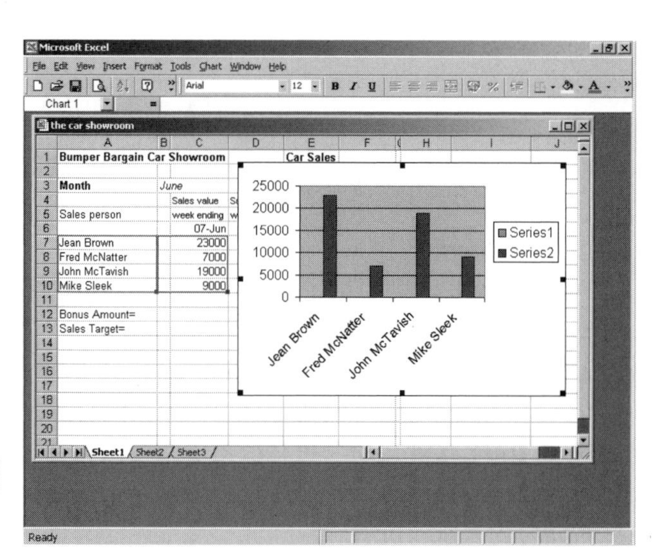

Numbers in a spreadsheet can be converted into a chart

Fig 2.26

Automatic and manual calculations

With *automatic calculation* turned on, your spreadsheet will calculate a formula automatically. With *manual calculation* turned on, the result of the formula will not be calculated automatically.

Relative referencing

If you use **relative referencing** when you copy a formula across a row or down a column, the formula will change relative to the cells you copy it to.

Absolute referencing

If you use **absolute referencing** you can lock the formula on to a cell. The formula will then refer back to the same cell no matter where you copy it to. Absolute referencing is usually indicated by using a $ symbol. See Figure 2.27.

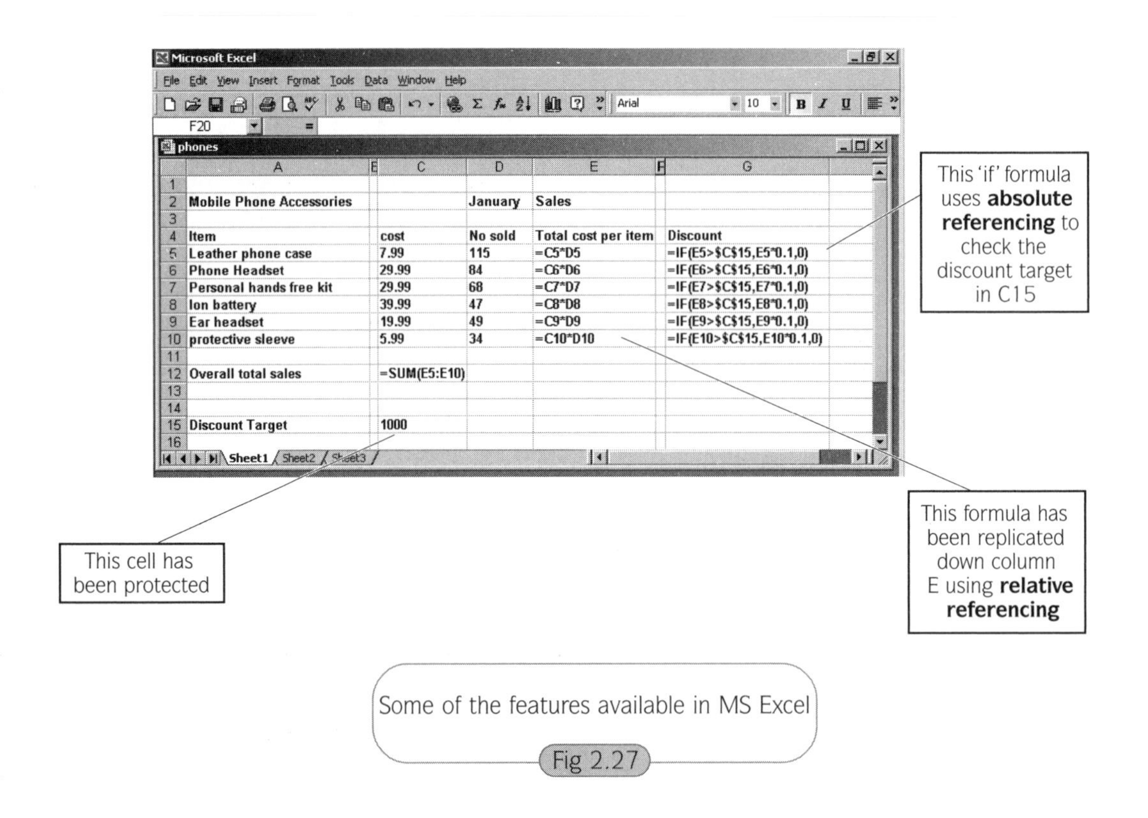

Some of the features available in MS Excel

Fig 2.27

Cell protection

You can lock a cell. This will prevent you from changing its value by accident, as in Figure 2.27.

Formula using conditions

A formula can contain a condition, such as 'If . . .'. An example of a condition is If(condition, true,false), as in If(A4>50,"pass","fail"), this means that if cell **A4** has a **value greater than 50** then '**pass**' is displayed in the cell where the formula has been entered, if not then '**fail**' is displayed.

Fully labelled charting

Your chart is fully labelled when it has a complete set of text labels such as the following:

- a label for the chart series
- a title for each individual chart
- a label for the x and y axes
- a label for each point on a chart showing its relation to the data.

Next steps continued

Microsoft Excel uses a wizard to help you through this process. Figure 2.28 shows one of Excel's Wizard windows outlining how to set up a label for a series of charts. This is very useful if you are producing a series of related charts on one subject. In the screenshot the series is labelled 'grades'.

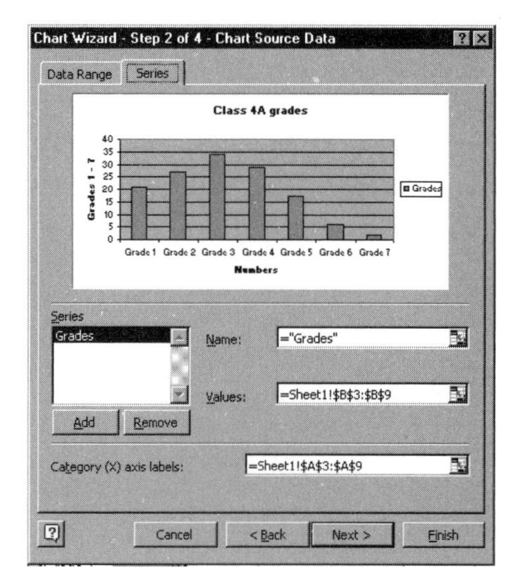

An Excel wizard window
Fig 2.28

Following the steps set out in the wizard will give you a fully labelled chart like the one in Figure 2.29.

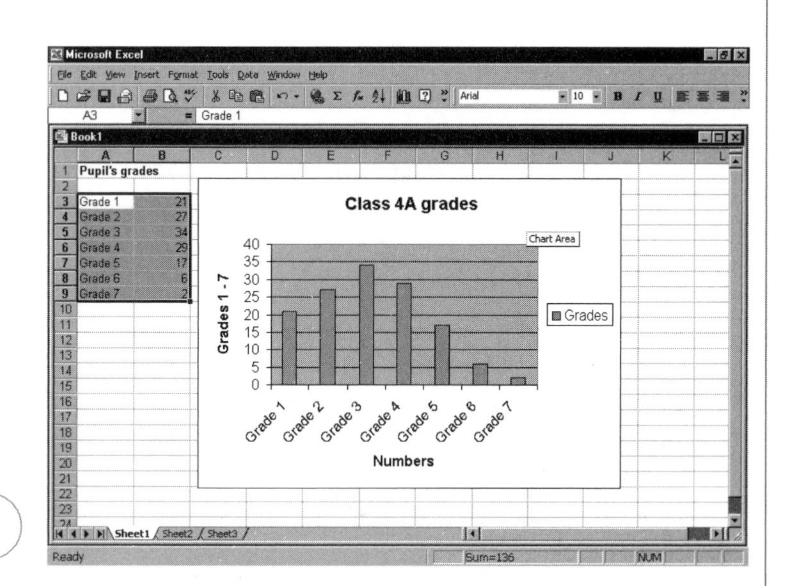

A result of using the Excel wizard
Fig 2.29

Now you try

List the labels that a fully labelled chart should have.

Now you try

Spreadsheet practical task

Create a spreadsheet to hold data on the results for A. Sellers, a computer salesman (Figure 2.30).

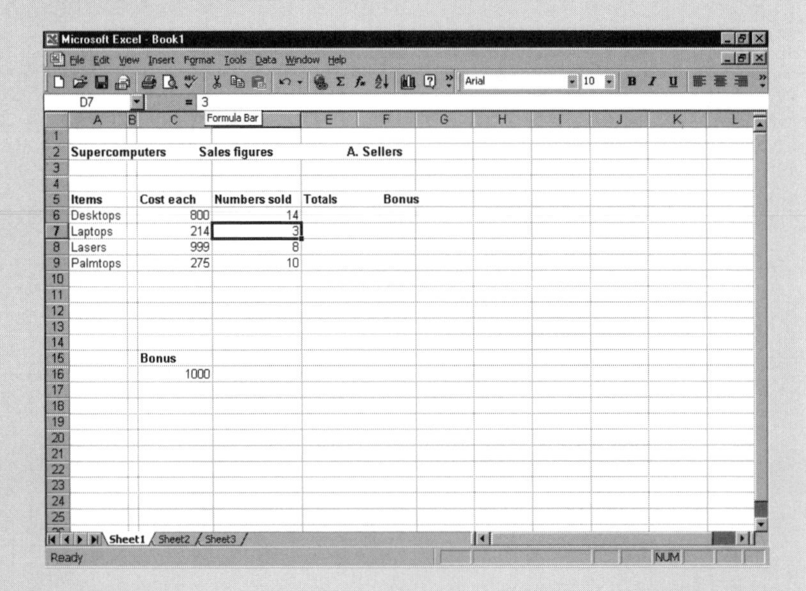

	A	C	D	E	F
2	Supercomputers	Sales figures		A. Sellers	
5	Items	Cost each	Numbers sold	Totals	Bonus
6	Desktops	800	14		
7	Laptops	214	3		
8	Lasers	999	8		
9	Palmtops	275	10		
15		Bonus			
16		1000			

Data for the spreadsheet practical task

Fig 2.30

1. Change the attributes of the cells so that they display currency.
2. Note that the items are in alphabetical order. Insert a row to hold the following data: Inkjet printers £750.
3. Enter the formula to calculate the totals for the desktops.
4. Replicate the formula down column E.
5. Chart the total sales in column E.

Credit questions

6. Make sure the chart is fully labelled.
7. Mr Sellers will get a bonus for each item for which the total sales are above £5000. In cell F6 enter the formula to calculate the bonus for desktops.
8. Replicate the formula down the column using absolute reference.
9. Protect the cell holding the amount of the bonus.
10. Save your spreadsheet and print it out, as well as the chart.

Features of database applications

Records, fields and files

Databases are made up of **files**, which contain **records** which, in turn, are made up of **fields** (Figure 2.31).

So **files** are collections of records on a subject. Your teacher probably stores the results of the assessments for your class in a database file. Records hold all the fields on a particular object. There will be a record for each pupil in the class file. Fields hold items of data: each pupil's record will have a field for each assessment recorded.

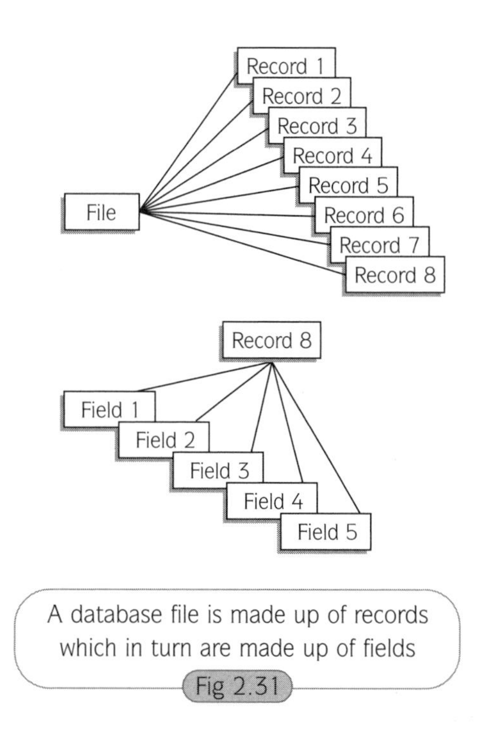

A database file is made up of records which in turn are made up of fields

Fig 2.31

Now you try

Using Figure 2.31 as a guide, draw the design for part of your class database file. Include about half a dozen records and all of the fields.

Adding records and creating fields

Once a database is set up you can add or delete records as you need to. You can also set up the fields in a record. You can set up fields to hold particular types of data, for example:

- numeric fields
- text fields
- graphic fields
- date
- time.

Searching and sorting on one field

You need to know how to search through the records using one field (e.g. to search on the *address field* for *Glasgow*). You also need to be able to sort the records into order based on one field (e.g. sorting into alphabetical order on the *name field*).

Carrying out simple searches using either a CD-ROM or the Internet

CD-ROMs are often used to hold information; an example is the CD-based encyclopaedia Encarta. Such an encyclopaedia will hold text, graphics, audio and video clips.

A simple search

The encyclopaedia will have a **search engine** which will let you search for things with a simple text entry in a **search box** – for example 'FIND: castle'. This would give you hundreds of castle entries, most of which you would not want.

You can also carry out simple searches using a search engine like Yahoo.

Search on more than one field

Searching for a record can be more precise if you use two fields (e.g. search on the ***surname*** field for 'McDonald' and on the ***forename*** field for 'Evelyn' and on the ***class*** field for '4/3' (Figure 2.32).

Sort on more than one field

Figure 2.33 shows an example of using two fields to sort records.

Next steps

More complex searches

Sometimes you need to carry out a complex search. Then you set up *conditions* which the search has to meet. You can set up a complex search with a condition in it to make your search more accurate – for example 'FIND: Edinburgh AND castle NOT military tatoo'.

The more conditions you put into your search, the more refined it will be and the more accurate – the conditions include exactly what you want and exclude things you do not want to search for.

For more information on searching, see the Communications and networks unit on page 12.

More information on databases

Altering a record format

You must be able to change the field type so that it can hold numbers and not text, for example.

Altering input and output formats

You must be able to change the appearance of the input screen from card form to columns, and to change the way the output is displayed (e.g. column or card output format).

Computed field

Computed fields hold formulae that carry out calculations on other fields in the database.

Keywords

A keyword is a unique identifier which is held in a keyfield. In a database used by a bank, the keyword would be the account number.

Next steps continued

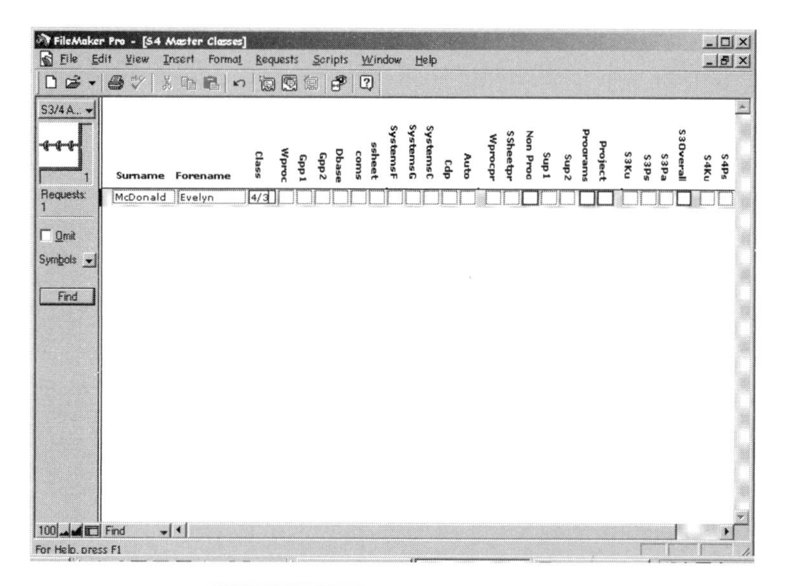

Searching a database using more than one field

Fig 2.32

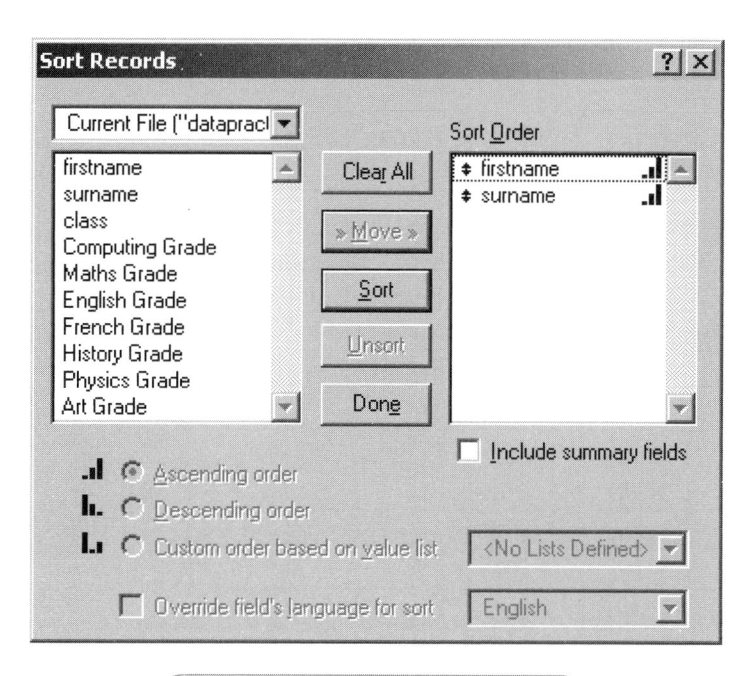

Sorting a database using more than one field

Fig 2.33

Next steps continued

Now you try

1. What is the main reason for using complex searches?
2. Why should you include as many conditions as you can in your search?
3. Write out the combination of conditions you would use to find out about Scottish islands in the Inner Hebrides *except* Mull or Coll. Carry out the search.

Now you try

Database practical task

Set up a database to hold the grades for ten pupils in class 4/2 and ten pupils in class 4/3. Each record should have fields holding the first name, the surname, the class and seven fields for grades. Table 2.2 shows you the pupils' names and grades.

Table 2.2 Information for the database practical task

Class 4/2	
James Macduff	Computing 2, Maths 2, English 1, French 4, Art 3, History 1, Physics 2
Jean Hamilton	Computing 1, Maths 4, English 1, French 1, Art 3, History 1, Physics 2
Eric McKenzie	Computing 3, Maths 2, English 1, French 1, Art 3, History 1, Physics 1
Habib Basra	Computing 1, Maths 2, English 1, French 2, Art 4, History 1, Physics 4
Mary McConnel	Computing 1, Maths 2, English 1, French 1, Art 5, History 1, Physics 3
Margaret Kelly	Computing 2, Maths 1, English 3, French 3, Art 3, History 1, Physics 2
Robert Benson	Computing 3, Maths 1, English 1, French 4, Art 4, History 1, Physics 4
Michael Poliri	Computing 2, Maths 3, English 1, French 4, Art 1, History 2, Physics 3
Rachel Logan	Computing 1, Maths 1, English 1, French 4, Art 2, History 1, Physics 1
David Watt	Computing 1, Maths 2, English 1, French 2, Art 1, History 1, Physics 1

Class 4/3	
John Jeffries	Computing 1, Maths 2, English 1, French 3, Art 3, History 1, Physics 2
Gavin McTavish	Computing 2, Maths 1, English 1, French 4, Art 2, History 4, Physics 3
Bill McLaren	Computing 2, Maths 3, English 2, French 5, Art 1, History 2, Physics 2
Peter O'Sullivan	Computing 2, Maths 2, English 3, French 2, Art 3, History 1, Physics 2
Mary McDonald	Computing 1, Maths 2, English 1, French 4, Art 5, History 1, Physics 2
Fiona Stevenson	Computing 2, Maths 2, English 4, French 1, Art 3, History 2, Physics 2
Jocelyn McJimpsey	Computing 3, Maths 2, English 1, French 3, Art 2, History 3, Physics 2
Bill Wallace	Computing 1, Maths 5, English 3, French 4, Art 3, History 1, Physics 2
Alex McFarlane	Computing 4, Maths 2, English 1, French 4, Art 3, History 3, Physics 2
Alan Youlsh	Computing 2, Maths 2, English 4, French 4, Art 3, History 1, Physics 2

The records should appear as in Figure 2.34.

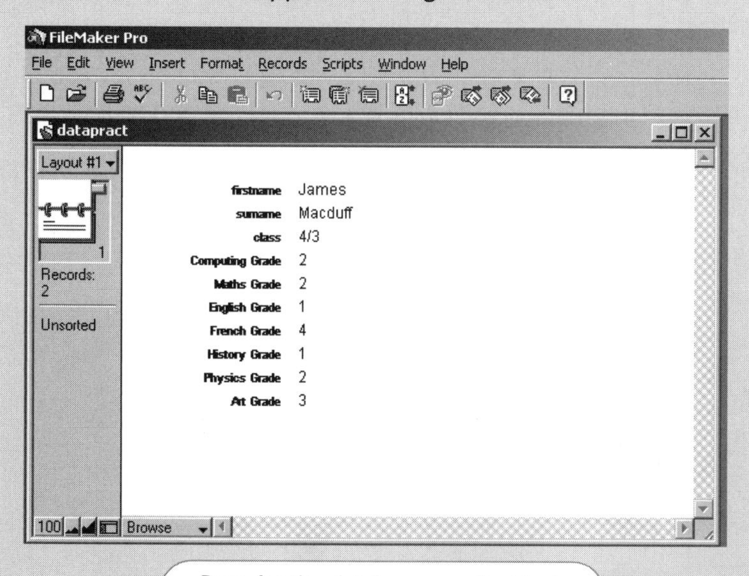

Data for the database practical task

Fig 2.34

Now do the following:

1 Add a record for a new pupil.
2 Search on the name field for the record for the pupil John Jeffries and print it out.

3 Sort the file into order of their scores in Art. Print out the list.
4 Add a new field to hold a grade for Chemistry.

Credit questions

5 Search for all pupils who scored grade 2 or above in both French and Computing. Print out the list.
6 Sort the file into order of their grades in computing and their surnames.
7 Add a key field to hold a unique identifier: a pupil number, in the range 1–20. Search for pupil 18. Print out the record.
8 Add a computed field to calculate and store the average grade for each pupil. Insert the correct formula to calculate each pupil's average grade. Print out a list of pupils sorted on the average field and the surname field.

Features of graphics applications

Entering text

Entering text is useful in a graphics application. It is used to label and explain drawings.

Selecting a tool and its attributes

Graphics applications have a range of tools for drawing lines, circles and rectangles, as well as for shading and colouring objects. You can change the properties of a tool by, for example, making a line thicker.

Scaling and rotating

- **Scale**. This lets you change the graphic image by altering its height and/or its width.
- **Rotate**. You can also turn your image around to view it at another angle.

Figure 2.35 shows an example of this.

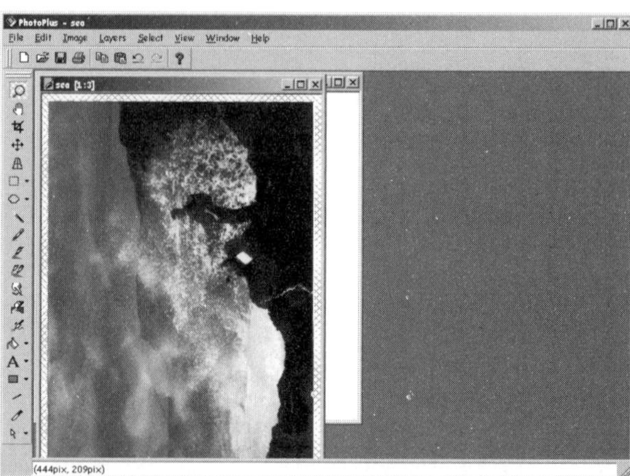

A graphics application allows images to be rotated for example

Fig 2.35

Next steps

Scanning a graphic image

To scan a graphic image you have to load up the scanning software and then choose some settings. These give you control of how the graphic is to be scanned. You have various options. You can choose:

- the resolution of the scan
- the number of bits used to store each pixel, which affects the number of colours in the graphic and the file size
- the format of the file in which the graphic is saved.

Editing a scanned image

Once a graphic image has been scanned you can open it up in a graphics application and begin to edit it. The extent to which you can edit the image depends on the sophistication of your software. Common editing features are: crop; rotate; scale; adjust colours; layer on to other graphic objects; zoom in/out; add special effects (Figures 2.36 and 2.37).

Cropping a graphic

To *crop* is to select a part of a graphic you want to keep. In most applications the area of the graphic not selected is not lost or discarded immediately; it is hidden and can be recovered if you change your mind before saving the modified image file. In Figure 2.36, part of the background is being cropped, leaving the tree in the loch more central in the image.

Cropping a graphic image

Fig 2.36

A graphics application usually offers many effects, chosen from a menu

Fig 2.37

Now you try

1 You scan a graphic and insert it into your Web page. When completed, the page looks good but probably takes a long time to load. What changes to the graphic can you make to speed up the loading process?

2 Do you have software which allows you to edit scanned graphics? If so, list six of its editing features.

Now you try

Word processing, database and graphics practical task

Credit questions

1 Produce a *standard letter*. The letter should ask people to take part in a questionnaire. You can encourage them by saying that returned questionnaires will automatically entitle the sender to be entered in a prize draw. Make sure you leave spaces in the text to personalise the letter as much as possible when it is printed. At the end include a short questionnaire.
2 At the top of the letter, insert a logo using a drawing you have produced yourself. Experiment with the graphic by *scaling* it and *rotating* it until you are satisfied with its size and position.
3 Save the standard letter to your hard disk.
4 Set up a database file holding five names.
5 Set up a mail merge.
6 Print out five letters.

You may need to use the help files of your word processing and database applications to find out how to do a mail merge. You could also ask your teacher for instructions.

Desktop publishing

A desktop publishing application is one which helps you set up documents that combine text and graphics. It helps you to place text and graphics in your document with great precision. Many DTP packages use vertical and horizontal rulers and guideline grids to help you.

Most DTP software uses **wizards** to help you get started. The wizard in Figure 2.38 is helping the user to set up a document by producing a template with a large heading.

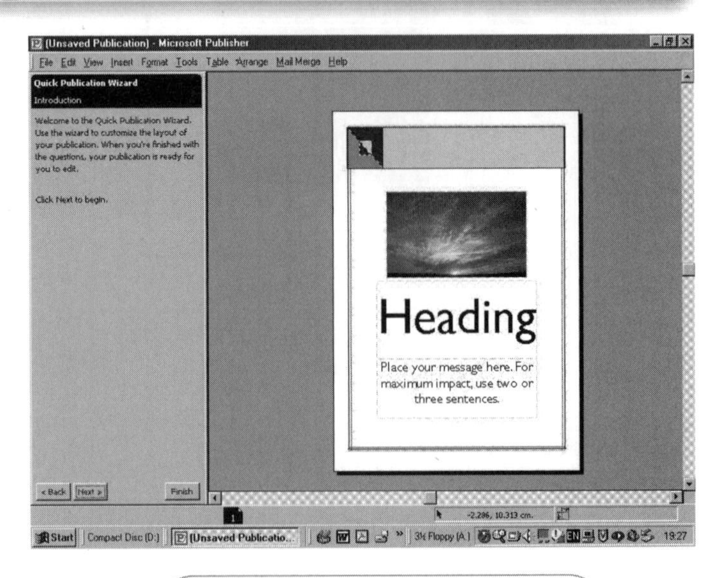

Using a wizard in MS Publisher, a desktop publishing application

Fig 2.38

Importing other graphics files

You may want to bring in graphics which you have produced using a graphics application or from a digital camera or scanner. Your DTP software will let you do this very simply by asking you to select which file you want to be inserted (Figure 2.39).

Once the graphic is in place it is a simple matter to scale it (see page 54).

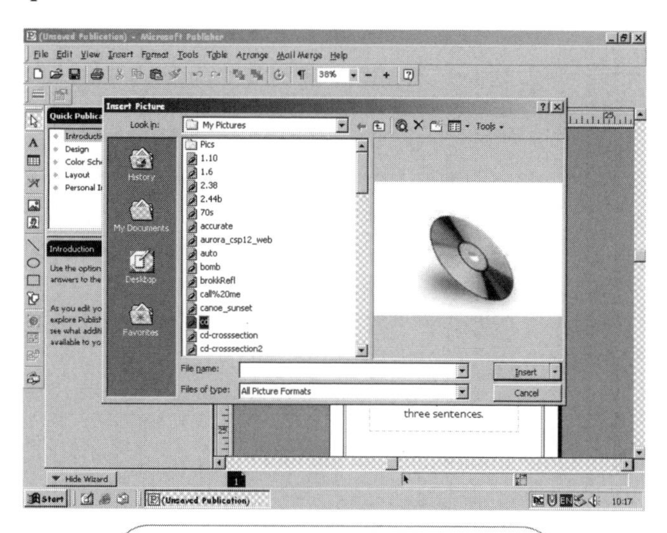

Importing a graphics file into a DTP application

Fig 2.39

Next steps

Importing text

Once your graphic is in place you can set up a text frame and pour in your text, which has been previously written in a word processing application. The procedure for doing this is similar to that for importing a graphic.

At this point you can, if you want to, change the **layout** of your document by altering the positions of text frames and graphic objects using the precise control which comes with desktop publishing applications (Figure 2.40).

Text wrap

This faciliy enables you to let your text flow around a graphic.

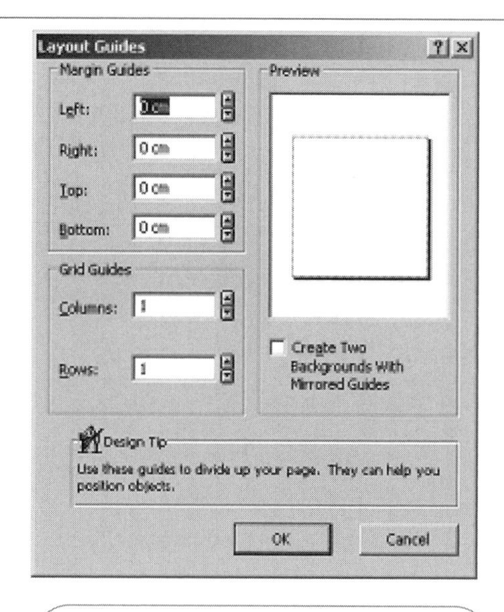

Changing the layout of a DTP document

Fig 2.40

Wrapping text around graphics

Fig 2.41

Next steps continued

Now you try

1 Using a desktop publishing application, choose a template for a document.
2 Use the template to produce the document and record how the template helps you.
3 Import a graphic into your document. What does importing a graphic mean?
4 Crop the graphic and explain how this improves the document.
5 Find out about and use the features of your DTP application which can help you (a) position your text and graphics with precision, and (b) alter the layout.

Presentation and multimedia

Presentation and multimedia software allows you to set up exciting and attractive documents which help you get your message across and capture your audience's imagination. A wizard will guide you through the process of entering text and adding images. If your software does not have a wizard then your teacher will be your wizard and give you a template which you can use to enter your own text and graphics.

Linear linkage of slides

Once you have made up your pages you need to begin to link them together. Some applications such as PowerPoint automatically set up simple links between slides so that they follow one after another. To move to the next slide all you have to do is click. Figure 2.42 shows a set of slides linked in this way.

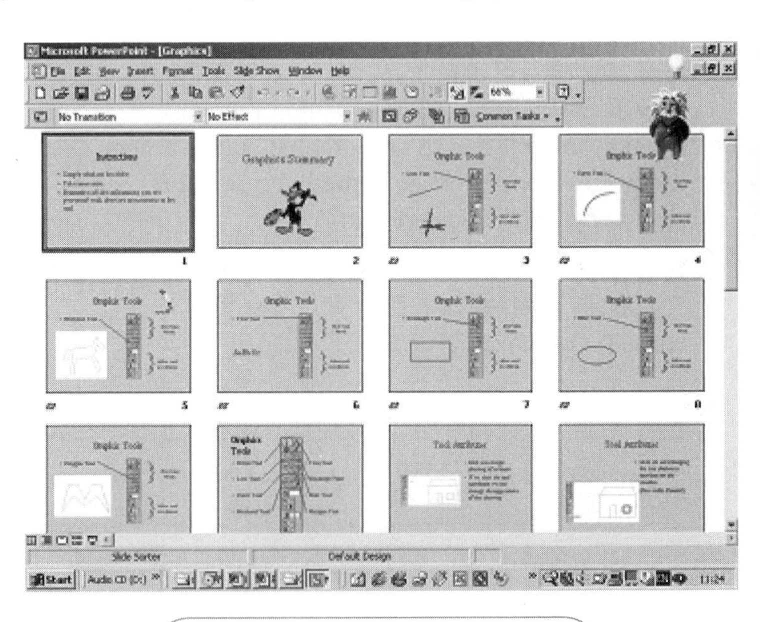

Linking slides in MS PowerPoint, a presentation application

Fig 2.42

Adding audio to your multimedia document

Once you have set up your pages you can attach an audio file to a slide in a presentation, and in some packages to an object on the page. This is usually a simple matter of pointing at the location of the audio file (Figure 2.43).

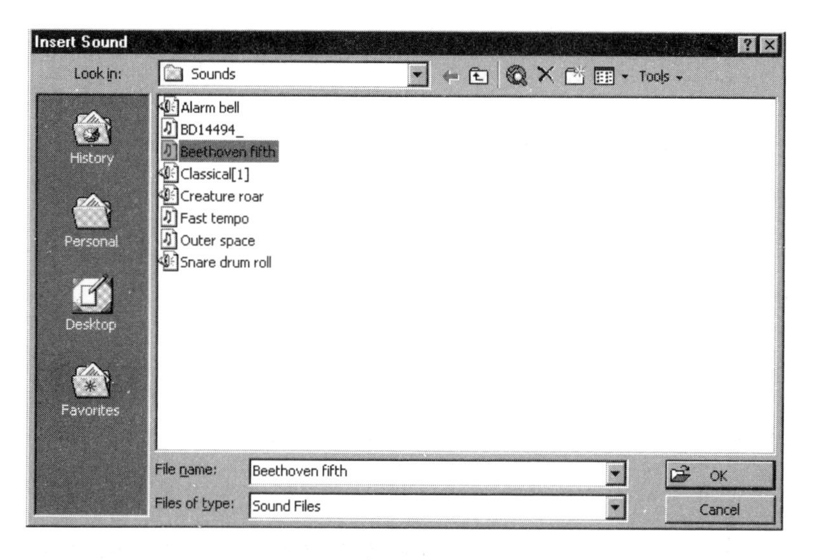

Adding audio to your multimedia document

Fig 2.43

Assembling elements of a presentation

Using the editing features of your software you can assemble all of the elements of your document and lay them out exactly as you want them on the page. The page shown in Figure 2.44 has text, a graphic, buttons and boxes to display a score.

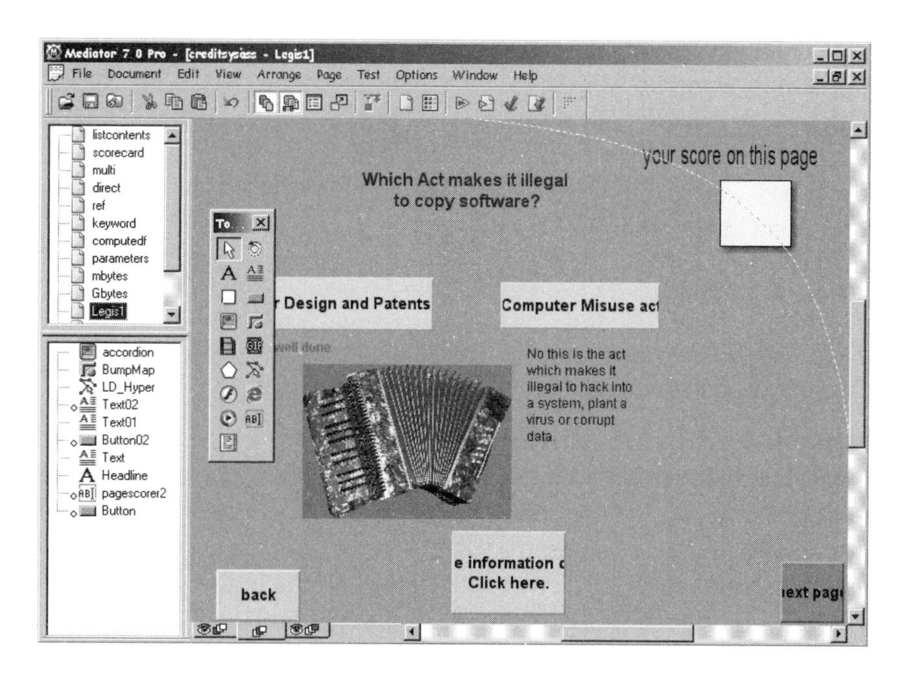

You can use your design skills to place elements on a page

Fig 2.44

Adding video

Video clips are an integral part of a good multimedia presentation. The clips, often saved as mpeg files, are easily linked into a document.

Common steps involved in adding a video clip to your document are:

- set up a frame to hold the video
- show the software where the file is stored in your hierarchical folder structure.

Some packages even have template frames available for you to use with videos with forward, reverse, pause and play buttons.

Next steps

Capturing audio

You might want to capture your own sounds to include them in your presentation by recording a piece of music from an audio CD, recording your voice using a microphone, or linking your computer up to a MIDI keyboard. You can then store these audio files in a directory and link them to a page in your document or to an object in the document (e.g. a button).

Recording your voice is a simple procedure. Most desktops have a sound recorder facility like the one in Figure 2.45.

To accurately capture any sophisticated sounds (e.g. from a CD player) you will need to have a good sound card in your computer. For more information on sound cards see page 120.

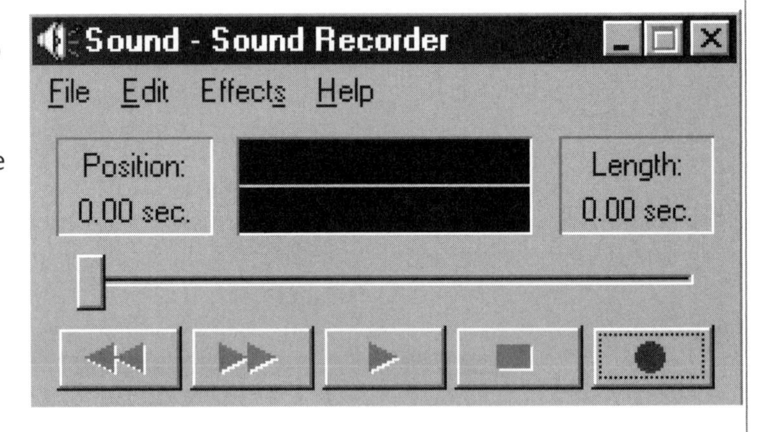

Sounds can be recorded for your multimedia document

Fig 2.45

Capturing images

You may want to capture your own images to incorporate into your multimedia or presentation document. The most common ways of doing this are:

- using a digital camera
- using a scanner
- downloading an image from the Internet.

To find out more about using a digital camera or a scanner, see page 115. You may even want to add a video clip to your multimedia document.

Using hyperlinks to link slides

Sometimes when you are setting up a multimedia presentation you want the user to be able to take different paths through the material. This makes the presentation more interactive.

There are two common ways of doing this:

- give the user a menu made up of hyperlinks, showing the options available (Figure 2.46a).
- include buttons on a page, so users can select their route (Figure 2.46b).

Next steps continued

Intermediate 2 Revision

Click on the topic to do the exercise. Let your teacher see your score and then correct any errors

- Memory
- Peripherals
- Systems Software
- Programming Languages
- Applications
- Input devices
- Output devices
- Backing Storage devices
- Systems Quiz

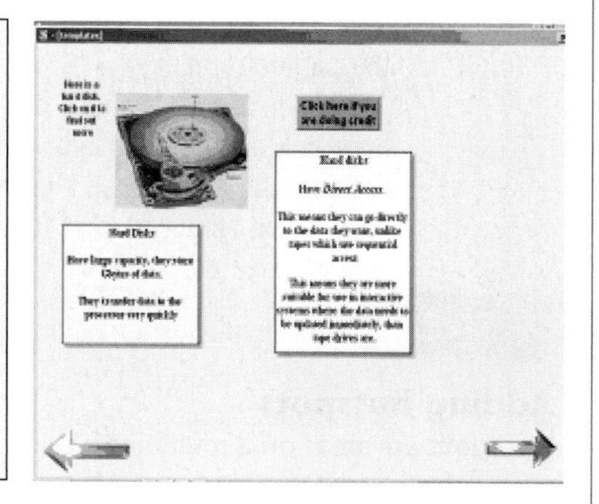

Users can be given options about navigating through the presentation

Fig 2.46

Web page creation

Many applications which help you set up Web pages have templates designed to get you off to a good start. Figure 2.47 shows a series of templates for frame pages which you use in Microsoft's FrontPage as the starting point for your website.

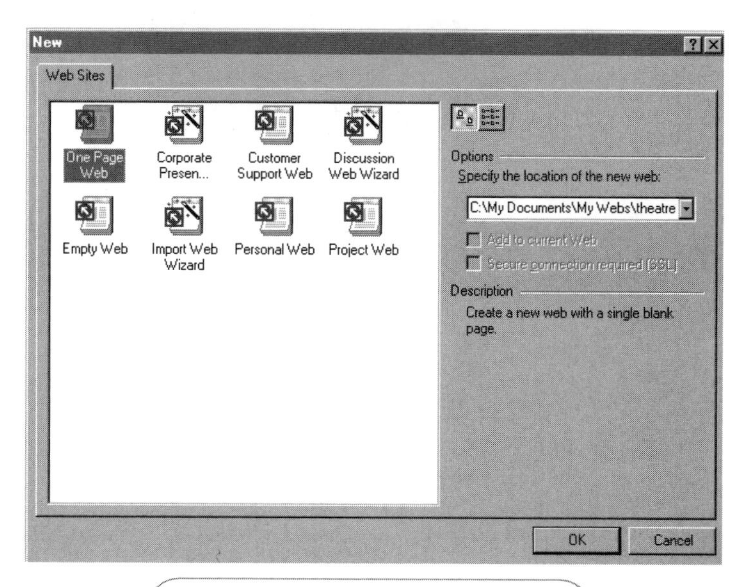

Web page creation the simple way

Fig 2.47

Entering text and adding graphics images

You can either enter text directly on to your page or use a table. A table is a very useful way of controlling the position of text and graphics on a Web page. Adding images is a similar process to adding graphics to a DTP document.

Adding simple linkage between pages

You can set up simple links to navigate between your Web pages. The easiest way of linking your pages is to have them set out one after another, so that one page is linked to the page after it.

You can link your pages by setting up hyperlinks. It is quite straightforward to add a hyperlink, simply choose to insert a hyperlink and then browse for the page you want to link through to. You can choose a range of objects to link you to the next page. You can have a text link, a graphic link, or a link button that uses a graphic as an icon.

Next steps

Adding hotspots

Hotspots are areas on a multimedia page which let the user interact with the page. When the user moves the cursor into a hotspot, or clicks on it, this action triggers an event – like loading another page or activating a sound file. This effect gives the page interactivity, lets the user have a choice as to what happens next, and brings your page alive and makes it more attractive. An example is shown in Figure 2.48.

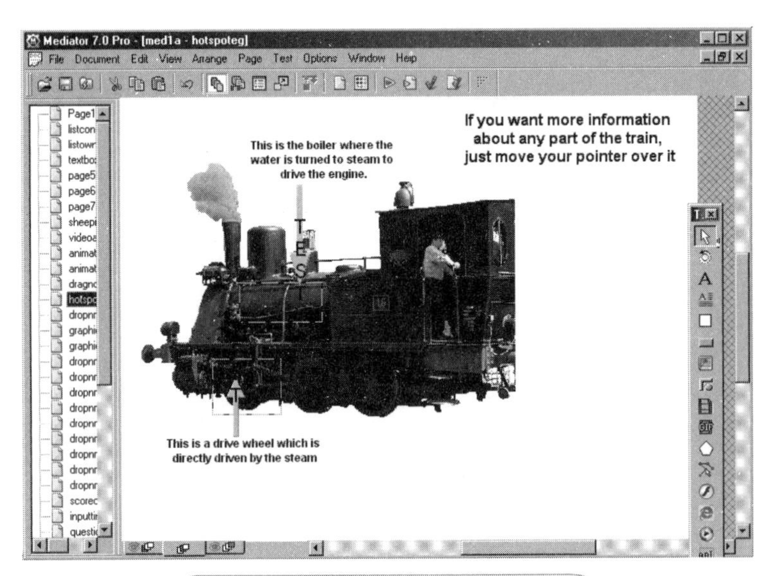

This image contains two hotspots: when the cursor is moved over a hotspot the associated arrow and text appear on the page

Fig 2.48

Adding tables

When creating Web pages, tables are very useful for keeping text and graphics together. You can then drop text and graphics into the cells of the table.

Next steps continued

Now you try

1. Plan and implement a simple website/multimedia presentation on a topic of your choice (e.g. a pop group, friends and family, your favourite sport).
2. Think carefully about the following before you start building your website:
   (a) where and why you would use simple sequential linkage of pages/slides?
   (b) why you might want to link your slides or pages in a more complex way?
   (c) what effect the process of having several pathways through your presentation will have on the user?
   (d) where would it be best to add tables and hotspots?

Expert systems

Expert systems are an application of artificial intelligence (AI) to a particular area of activity where traditional human expert knowledge are made available through a computer package.

An expert system is made up of:

- a *knowledge base* which holds the facts about a subject, provided by an expert
- a *rule base*, which are analytical rules defined by an expert in the subject
- an *HCI* which lets the user put questions to the system
- an *inference engine*, which is software that searches the knowledge base, answers the query, and then offers explanations to the user of the reasoning behind the answer it gives.

What is an expert system used for?

- *In medicine*. Doctors and nurses can find out what is wrong with a patient.
- *In equipment repair*. The software helps to find and fix faults with complex machines.
- *In investment analysis*. People can work out how to invest their money.
- *In the insurance business*. Insurance companies can work out risks and the size of premiums.
- *In vehicle routing*. Travellers can find their way about the road system avoiding jams.
- *In production control*. Managers in factories keep the production lines moving smoothly.

Next steps

Advantages of Expert Systems

- The user has rapid access to the knowledge of an expert in the subject. This helps people to make complicated and important decisions quickly without having to have a human expert on hand.
- People can learn about a subject by asking questions and then analysing the reasons given by the expert system for the advice given.

Mid-unit progress check on application packages

You have reached the end of the applications packages part of the general-purpose packages topic. It is a good idea to check your knowledge of these packages and to do some problem-solving before moving on to the next section.

Spreadsheet

Look carefully at the spreadsheet in Figure 2.49. It shows the amounts sold by a group of sales people each week in June. Notice that the records are in *alphabetical order,* and that there are places for *bonuses* and *amounts*. Business is so good that an extra salesperson, Margaret Lawson, has been employed.

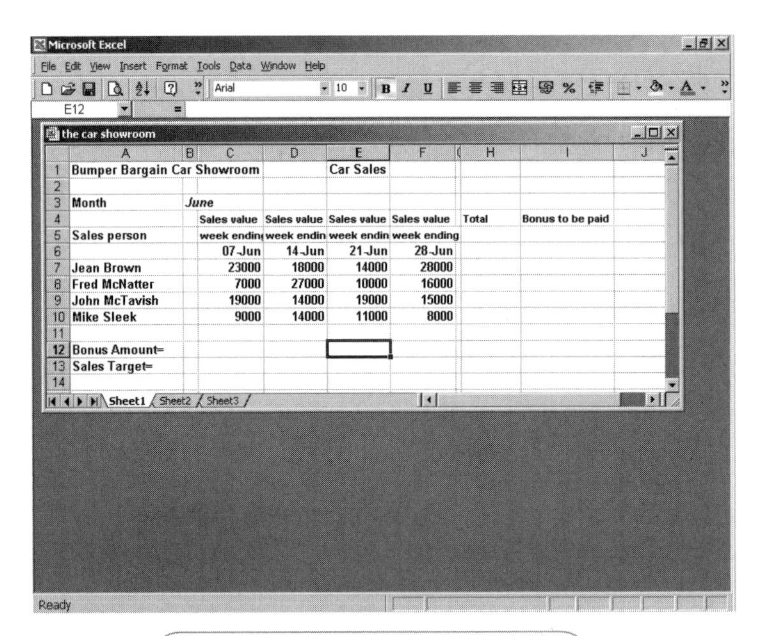

	A	B	C	D	E	F	H	I
1	Bumper Bargain Car Showroom				Car Sales			
2								
3	Month	June						
4			Sales value	Sales value	Sales value	Sales value	Total	Bonus to be paid
5	Sales person		week endin	week endin	week endin	week ending		
6			07-Jun	14-Jun	21-Jun	28-Jun		
7	Jean Brown		23000	18000	14000	28000		
8	Fred McNatter		7000	27000	10000	16000		
9	John McTavish		19000	14000	19000	15000		
10	Mike Sleek		9000	14000	11000	8000		
11								
12	Bonus Amount=							
13	Sales Target=							
14								

Data for the spreadsheet progress check

Fig 2.49

Foundation/general questions

1. For the first four weeks Margaret's sales records are kept on paper. At the end of the month they have to be entered into the spreadsheet. What has to be done so that her sales details can be entered into the right place? **2**
2. Write out the formula that has to be entered to add up the sales totals for Brown. **2**
3. The totals formula has to be transferred to cells H7 to H10. How could this be done? **1**
4. All the cells from C7 to F10 have to be shown as British currency. What has to be done to show the pound sign (£)? **2**
5. What is the address of the cell holding McTavish's name? **1**
6. How could the data in the spreadsheet be output so that it could be understood at a glance? **1**
7. What could you do to prevent the contents of B12 being changed accidentally? **1**

Foundation/general total **10 marks**

Credit questions

8 If a salesperson sells a total of over £60,000 worth of cars per month, he or she is given a bonus of £1000. Here is the formula the operator enters into cell I7: If(F2>60000;0;1000). Jean complains because her bonus is wrong. Write down the correct formula and give the reasons for the changes you have made. 3

9 The amount of the bonus is to be stored in cell B12. Change the formula, and column B, to take account of this. 1

10 Why does this last change make it easier to update the spreadsheet? 1

11 The formula for the bonus is now replicated down column I. Only the first bonus is correct.

(a) What is needed to remedy this? 1

(b) Write out the formula with the necessary changes. 2

12 How could you improve this formula further? 2

Credit total 10 marks

Database

Table 2.3 shows a record from a database file which holds all the grades for fourth-year pupils. Examine it carefully.

Table 2.3

Field name	*Contents of field*
Surname	Johnstone
First name	Mhairi
Class	4c
DOB	12/12/87
Systems grade	2
GPP grade	3
CDP grade	3
AS grade	2
Practical grade	2

Foundation/general questions

1 How many fields are in each record? 1

2 How should the teacher update the file when a new pupil joins the class ? 1

3 The teacher wants to keep a grade for programming. What needs to be done to the file? 1

4 What is the quickest way for the teacher to find Mhairi's record? 2

5 The teacher wants to see all the pupils' records in alphabetical order. How should this be done using the database? 2

6 The teacher wants to see as many as possible of the pupils' records on the screen at one time. How could she do this? 1

Foundation/general total 8 marks

7 The file holds records for two people called Mhairi Johnstone. How can the teacher find the correct record? 2

8 How can the database be used to get a list of all pupils in 4c who have scored grade 2 or above for Systems? 2

Credit questions

9 The teacher wants to keep a record of the pupils' average grade. Outline the steps needed to do this. 3

10 The teacher wants to find a quicker way to find pupils' records without having to carry out complex searches. What needs to be done to the file so that she can do this? 2

11 The teacher is not happy with the way the records are displayed on the screen. What can she do? 1

Credit total 10 marks

Word processing and graphics

Look carefully at the document in Figure 2.50.

Lochside Dwellings Ltd

To:

Date:

Dear

Excelsior Lunch Invitation

We are writing to invite you to a free lunch in the Excelsior Hotel next Wednesday evening 21st June. There you will be treated to a three course meal, free of charge, before being taken on an absolootely no strings attached tour of one of our time share lochside apartments each with own spectacular view of Ben Stramash.

I hope you can make it to the Excelsior next Wodnesday.

its

Yours sincerely

Alex Smoothey

Sales Manager

Lochside Dwellings Ltd

Document for the word processing and graphics progress check

Fig 2.50

Foundation/general questions

1	This letter needs to be amended. What does that mean?	1
2	What needs to be done with the word 'its'?	1
3	The spellchecker is going to be needed. How does it work?	2
4	The lunch venue is changed to the Hilton Hotel. How could the necessary changes to the letter be made without retyping?	1
5	The artist wants to make the drawing wider but not taller. What should she do?	2
6	Name *two* drawing tools that have been used in making the graphics.	2
7	The person who made this letter used a standard paragraph. Explain what a standard paragraph is.	2
	Foundation/general total	11 marks

Credit questions

8	This is an example of a standard letter. Write out *four* steps describing how it works.	4
9	What could be done to make it easier to create standard letters similar to this one in the future?	1
10	What additional application software might be used to produce a run of 100 of the standard letter?	1
11	The secretary deletes the standard letter file by accident, but has found a paper copy. How could she quickly replace the file and make any changes?	2
12	How would a template have helped the production of this document?	2
	Credit total	10 marks

Creating web pages and multimedia presentations

Foundation/general questions

1	How would a template help you set up a multimedia presentation?	2
2	What are hyperlinks?	1
3	Name two types of data, other than text and graphics, that you can include in a multimedia presentation.	2
	Foundation/general total	5 marks

Credit questions

4	Why are tables useful when putting Web pages together?	1
5	Describe two ways in which you could capture audio for a Web page.	2
6	Why are hotspots a useful addition to a Web page or multimedia presentation?	2
	Credit total	5 marks

Jobs, money, security and the law

Jobs, training and the working environment

When computers are introduced into a workplace, they affect peoples' jobs, change the environment they work in and create the need for training.

Jobs

Jobs are created for operators, maintenance engineers and systems analysts and programmers (there is information on commercial data processing on page 139). Computers can also make people's jobs redundant when humans are replaced by machines.

Training needs

When computer systems, complete with application software, are introduced the staff need to be trained. They will need to be trained to use a spreadsheet, a database, word processing, graphics, integrated packages, Web page creation software and multimedia authoring software. They also need training in the use of the hardware that makes up the system.

The cost of training is a short-term cost which can be very expensive. In the long term the increase in efficiency and the saving in staff time usually make the cost of training worthwhile.

Changes to the working environment

Offices might have to be redesigned because of health and safety requirements. Desks must be capable of holding computers as well as other working equipment. Chairs must be adjustable, and there must be proper ventilation and lighting. Special screens might be needed to cut down the glare and radiation from monitors.

More paper or a paperless world?

Does the use of computer applications to get work done mean that you don't need paper any more? There are two sides to this question.

On the one hand, lots of data is stored on hard disks and CDs and this reduces the amount of paper people have to deal with. On the other hand people still like to have printed copies of documents to read and check over. The fact that there are many good-quality laser and inkjet printers available means that people can produce very attractive and professional-looking documents quite easily – and this encourages them to make printed copies.

Using computer systems reduces the need to store large quantities of paper documents, but does not eliminate their use entirely.

Now you try

Write a couple of paragraphs answering these questions:

1. How would you rate the working environment you are working in just now? Do you have an adjustable chair? Is the room well lit and ventilated? Is your desktop on a suitable computer desk or bench?
2. What would need to be done to bring your work area up to standard?
3. Do you think that you produce less paperwork using your computer system, or is your printer always busy?

Initial costs, replacement costs and running costs

Initial costs

These are the costs at the beginning, when the computer system and general-purpose package are paid for. They are the costs of:

- buying and setting up the hardware and software
- buying furniture (e.g. adjustable chairs) and providing suitable ventilation and lighting
- the training courses.

Initial costs can be very high but are worth it in the long term since the computer system will make the business more efficient.

Replacement costs

Hardware and software will eventually need to be replaced, because:

- new improved software (e.g. a new operating system) will be developed
- new computers as well as peripherals such as printers and scanners will be available
- hardware such as printers will eventually wear out.

Running costs

These are the day-to-day costs, such as:

- staff salaries
- costs of maintaining the equipment
- cost of paper, ink cartridges for the inkjets and toner for the lasers
- cost of the telephone connections to a wide-area network (WAN) or the Internet.

Knowledge check 4

1. List *four* health and safety matters employees might be concerned about.
2. What could be done to put people's mind at rest.
3. Some people think that because you use computers you don't need paper any more. What do you think?
4. What is an initial cost? Give *two* examples in your answer.
5. What sort of training do people need when a computer system is introduced?

The law

Information held on computers and networks about people can be hacked into, and the data can be changed, copied or deleted. Thus, people's privacy can be invaded. Measures have to be taken to protect the data and people's rights.

In most cases people can ask to see the data held about them on a computer. There are *exceptions* to this. If the data is held by the Police, the security forces or the Inland Revenue the public is denied access.

Now you try

1. Find out what data about you your teacher holds on a computer.
2. Visit the data protection website and check out the documents stored there.

The Data Protection Act

The **Data Protection Act** was passed by parliament in 1984. It was updated in 1998 to make it comply with European law.

Data subjects – the people who have data held about them – have the following rights:

- to know whether data is held about them on a computer and to have a copy of the data
- to know why the data is being processed and who is going to receive the data
- to inspect that data and to have it changed if it appears to be inaccurate
- to ask for compensation if data is inaccurate or if an unauthorised person has been given access to it
- to prevent processing of data likely to cause damage or distress
- to be sure that decisions made about them are not made only on the basis of automatic processing (e.g. psychometric testing for jobs).

For all of these they can be charged a single fee. A data subject can also apply to the courts to block the processing of data or to correct, erase or destroy it.

Data Protection Register

Details about who holds information on members of the public on computer systems is held in the Data Protection Register which is to be found in central libraries.

Data Protection Commissioner

If anyone has a problem accessing data or has a complaint about the accuracy of data, the person can contact the office of the Data Protection Commissioner, who is in charge of administering the Act.

Data Controller

A Data Controller is the person, business or organisation controlling the collection, contents and use of personal data. The Data Controller must:

- register with the Data Protection Commissioner
- apply for permission to keep personal data on computers
- state what data they want to keep, what it will be used for and who has access to it.

The data controller must keep to the following data protection principles: All personal data should:

- be processed only if the consent of the individual is given, if it is part of a legal contract, and if it is essential to a business transaction or the carrying out of public duties
- be held for the specified purposes described in the Register entry
- be accurate and where necessary be kept up to date
- be relevant and not excessive in relation to the purpose for which it is held
- be adequate for the purpose specified
- be processed in accordance with the rights of the data subject
- be surrounded by proper security
- only be transferred to countries outside of the EU which have in place adequate security measures as defined in the act.

Data User

This is an authorised user within the organisation or business. A data user within a bank would be one of the bank's employees.

Next steps continued

Now you try

1 Who is the Data Controller for your school?
2 What security procedures protect the data held on your school's computers?

Knowledge check 5

Credit questions

1 Describe the rights people have to see data held about them on a computer system. What exceptions are there?
2 Who is the Data Protection Commissioner?
3 List *four* data protection principles which a data controller must stick to.
4 What is the Data Protection Register?
5 What is a data subject?
6 Who is a Data Controller?

The Computer Designs and Patents Act 1988

Software copyright is now protected by law for 50 years after it is published. This Act makes it illegal:

- to pirate software that is copyright protected
- to run pirated software
- to transmit software over telecommunications links and copy it.

The Computer Misuse Act 1990

This makes hacking into and damaging a computer system illegal and subject to penalties. This Act makes it illegal:

- to gain unauthorised access to a computer system (hacking)
- to make unauthorised modifications to computer materials.

The Act also covers *modifying computer material*, which means:

- interfering with a system so that it doesn't run properly (installing a virus)
- making changes to the system to prevent others gaining access (changing passwords)
- making changes to the software or data (altering the coding to make it carry out different operations or changing the contents of data files).

The penalties are up to five years' imprisonment and fines.

Precautions against loss or damage to data

Once data is stored in the computer system the data controller must *protect* it against loss or damage. This can be done by:

- setting up procedures to make regular backups of data, usually with multiple copies which are stored securely in different locations
- taking measures to prevent unauthorised persons 'hacking' into the system, changing the data, copying it or inserting viruses.

Data security measures

Physical security measures

- Fit security locks on computer rooms.
- Have security keys on computer workstations.
- Install workstations without disk drives.

System security measures

- Set up IDs and passwords for access to different levels of the system.
- Encode data (by encryption).
- Install anti-virus software.
- Use audit software to trace who has accessed accounts.
- Use advanced security systems to control access – such as fingerprints or voice recognition.

Knowledge check 6

1. What is the Computer Misuse Act designed to make illegal?
2. What is a hacker?
3. What is a virus?
4. What can you do to (a) prevent a virus getting into your computer, and (b) recover files that have been damaged?
5. List *two* security measures that can be used inside your computer system.
6. List *three* possible physical security measures.

Credit questions

7. List *three* things the Computer Designs and Patents Act is designed to make illegal.

End of unit progress check

You have reached the end of the general-purpose package topic. You have already checked your knowledge of applications packages (on page 64). It's now time to check your knowledge of the rest of this topic and to do some problem-solving.

Foundation/general level questions

1 Complete these sentences:
(a) General-purpose packages help you save ____ when searching for information.
(b) If you make backups properly, they help prevent ____ of data.
(c) You can use them to ___________ by creating documents and sending them to other people using computer networks.
(d) They can help reduce _____ in the long term, though they can be expensive to buy initially. 3

2 (a) What is a WIMP? 2
(b) Give *two* reasons why is it so user-friendly. 2

3 Your friend has a couple of problems. He has difficulty transferring data from his spreadsheet software to his word processor. He also finds each application has completely different menus and icons.
(a) Can you suggest a package he could buy to solve his problem? 1
(b) Give the reasons for your suggestion. 2

4 At work you have a new software package on your Desktop. Your boss doesn't have the money to pay for you to go on a training course. Is there any other way you could get to know how to use the package? 1

5 Your brother has just finished writing a large essay for his English teacher. What should he do to make sure the data is not lost? 1

6 A computer salesman visits your office and says that, by using one of his computers, you will not need to have any paper in your office, since all data will be stored on the hard disk. Is he correct? Give your reasons. 1

7 What changes have to be made to an office when a new computer is installed? 2

8 You apply for a loan and are refused because the bank's computer system says you are a bad risk. You don't agree. What can you do about it? 2

9 You are making a multimedia presentation for training purposes. How would adding audio improve your presentation? 1

Foundation/general total 18 marks

Credit questions

10 How would adding a hotspot to your Web page make it more interactive? 2

11 You have to send a text file to a friend. What would be the advantage of sending the file in RTF format rather than as an ASCII file? 2

12 You have to write a report on the sales of cars in your showroom. This combines text from a word processing file and numbers from a spreadsheet. The text in the report stays very much the same. What does change constantly are the figures and totals which you have transferred in from your spreadsheet file. How could you use your integrated package to make the process of producing the report easier? 2

13 You find that the integrated package you are using does not have all the features you need to do the report.

(a) How could you upgrade your integrated software? 1

(b) Why would you need to check the capacity of your system's main memory and backing storage? 1

14 Your company website has problems. The text has become separated from its associated graphics, and visitors to the site cannot find their way around the pages. What needs to be done? 2

15 One of your friends phones you up and tells you that she has just changed some of the HCI parameters on her computer. List *two* things she may have changed. 2

16 Your boss asks you to prepare a presentation for staff on the problems that the Data Protection Act might bring up. Write down *four* main points you would make in your talk. 4

17 Someone is caught hacking into your computer system. She has planted a virus and deleted some data files. Which law has she broken? 1

18 You are asked to e-mail a 40-page text document immediately. The person receiving the document will need to be able to edit it. You only have a paper copy. What should you do? 1

Credit total 18 marks

Unit 3

Automated systems

What you will read about in this unit

- What is an automated system?
- Why are automated systems used?
- A closer look at automated systems
- CAD and CAM
- Simulation
- Virtual reality
- The control of automated systems
  - Programs and high level language
  - The use of sensors
  - Embedded systems
  - Intelligent robots
- Analogue and digital signals
- Real-time processing
- The economics of automated systems
- Automated systems and people's jobs

What is an automated system?

When computers are used to control a system consisting of machinery and equipment, we call that an automated system. Automated systems are used for many things, such as:

- controlling machinery in factories
- controlling traffic lights
- guiding aircraft, trains and rockets.

Automated systems take many forms, the most common of which are **robots** (Figure 3.1).

Experimental robots

Fig. 3.1

Why are automated systems used?

- *They operate at high speed.* This makes them suitable for controlling machinery.
- *They can handle repetitive tasks without making mistakes.* Therefore they are suited to doing jobs on factory assembly lines.
- *They are accurate.* They follow the instructions in the software and don't make mistakes.
- *They can work in dangerous places where it is unsafe for people to work.* From nuclear power plants to outer space, automated systems are used where people would be in danger (Figure 3.2).

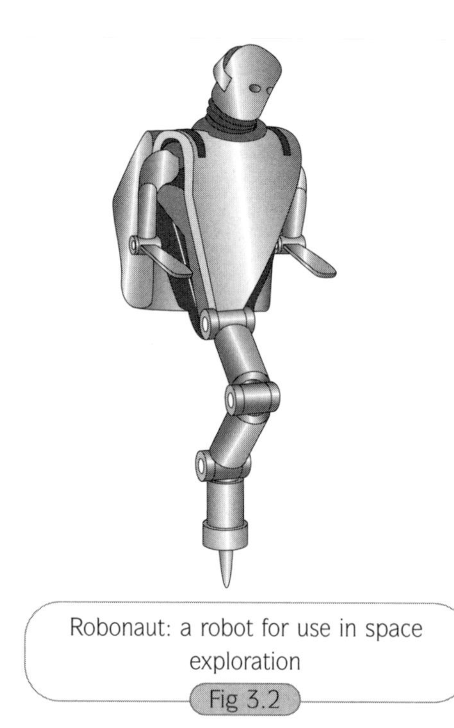

Robonaut: a robot for use in space exploration

Fig 3.2

Next steps

Automated systems are adaptable

This means that they can be used to perform a range of different jobs. What makes them adaptable is the fact that they can be re-programmed to carry out different jobs. A robot arm fitted with a spray gun spray-painting a line of Ford Focus cars can easily be adapted to paint a much larger and differently shaped car, such as a Ford Mondeo, simply by changing the program. Also, the appliance at the end of the robot arm can be changed to make it carry out an entirely different task, such as welding a car body.

Now you try

Here are five places you can find automated systems being used:

- a chemical factory
- the Glasgow Science Centre Tower (Figure 3.3)
- car factories
- in the North Sea oil industry
- in factories making microchips.

Take each in turn and, if you can, give a reason why the automated system is being used. For more information on the Science Centre Tower, see page 84.

The Glasgow Science Centre Tower

Fig 3.3

A closer look at automated systems

Stationary robots

These are robot arms that are fixed in one place. A good example is in a car factory where the robot arms are used to weld, spray-paint cars and lift objects. Robot arms have **mobile joints** called the *wrist*, the *elbow*, the *waist* and the *shoulder* (Figure 3.4).

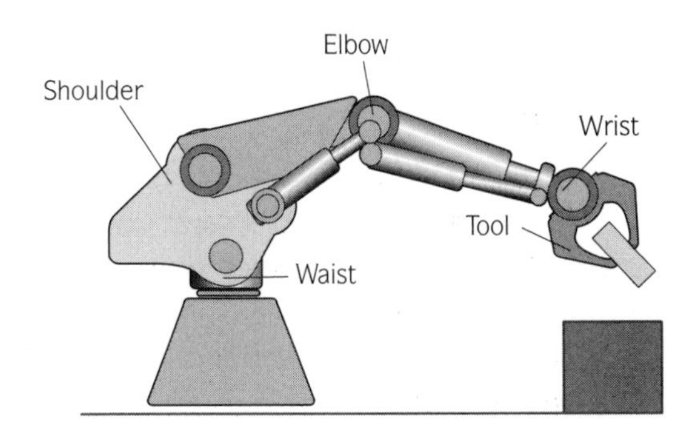

A stationary robot

Fig 3.4

Mobile robots

On land, mobile robots move around using wheels or tracks and are usually powered by electric motors. They are often used in dangerous places. Figure 3.5 shows a mobile robot that is used for research in the Antarctic.

A mobile robot used for research in the Antarctic

Fig 3.5

How mobile robots are guided

You need to know about two ways of guiding a mobile robot when it is working inside a factory: magnetic guidance and light guidance.

Magnetic guidance

The robot follows a magnetic field which comes from a cable buried in the floor. The robot uses sensors which detect the magnetic field and feed back the information about it to the processor which controls the robot's movements.

Light guidance

The robot follows a white line painted on the floor (Figure 3.6). It shines light on to the floor and then uses sensors to follow the light reflected back from the white line. The information about the line is fed back to the processor controlling its movements.

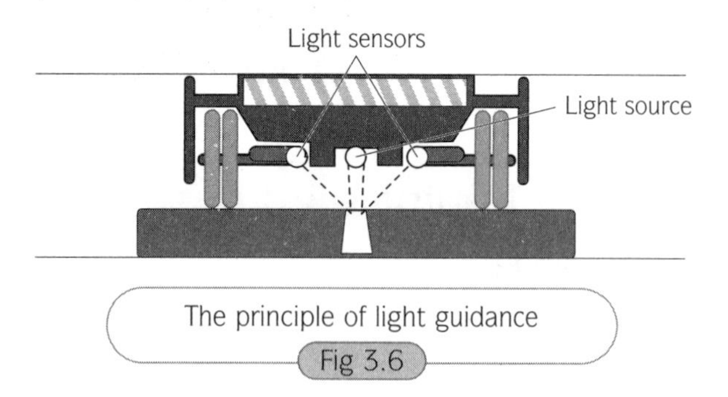

The principle of light guidance

Fig 3.6

Now you try

1 Which tasks do you think (a) a mobile robot and (b) a stationary robot could carry out in a car factory?
2 Which type of guidance system do you think would be easiest to install?
3 How would you describe the job of the sensor in these guidance systems?

CAD and CAM

CAD

CAD stands for **computer-aided design**. CAD systems are used by architects, planners and many others for making complicated designs and plans, for example of buildings and cars.

CAD systems are used because they make it much easier to produce complex drawings. Using a CAD system you can easily make changes to your drawing after it is finished, and making extra copies is simply a matter of sending them to the plotter.

CAD systems have high-resolution monitors and powerful processors and lots of backing storage. They also often have graphics tablets for input and a plotter for output (Figure 3.7).

A high-resolution monitor, plotter and graphics tablet

Fig 3.7

CAM

CAM stands for **computer-aided manufacture**.

In industry many factories use computers to control machinery. A good example of this are computer numerically controlled (**CNC**) machines which are used to cut complex objects from metal. CNC machines will cut object after object repeatedly with extremely high accuracy. See Figures 3.8 and 3.9.

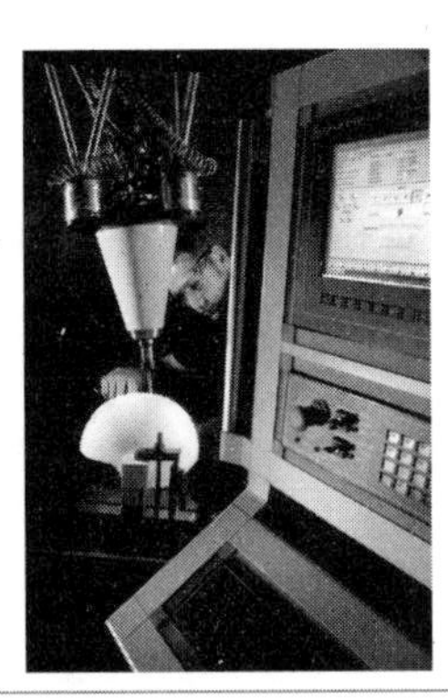

An object produced accurately using computer guidance

Fig 3.8

Robot arms used in computer-aided manufacture in a car factory

Fig 3.9

Some industries have integrated CAD/CAM systems. Parts are designed using a CAD system, and these designs are then fed directly to the computer controlling the machinery and robots are used to cut out the parts and assemble the finished product.

Simulation

Simulation is the use of a computer to create a model of, for example, flying a plane or driving a car. Computer-based models can be used for simulation games or for training people. You can, for example, use simulators to learn how to drive a car or a train or fly a plane.

In a simple simulator the computer takes in the user's control signals, processes them and sends an output to a screen. This helps people to develop their skills without the danger or expense of the real thing.

Virtual reality

Using a headpiece with stereo vision screens, speakers and sensors, a virtual reality system allows the user to enter the virtual world of the computer, move around inside it and manipulate it.

This means that virtual worlds can be created:

- to train people in using and maintaining sophisticated machines
- to examine CAD models from the inside.

For example, once a car or a plane has been designed, the designer can enter the virtual model and inspect the design from the inside before it has even been built.

Find out more about virtual reality systems on page 122.

Knowledge check 1

1. Give *four* reasons for using automated systems.
2. Describe a stationary robot.
3. Give *one* use for a stationary robot in a car factory.
4. Give an example of what a mobile robot might be used for.
5. How does a light guidance system work?
6. Describe a CAD system.
7. What is CAM?
8. Give *two* examples of the tools that can be fitted to the end of a robot arm.

Credit question

9. What is it that makes automated systems adaptable?

The control of automated systems

Software (a computer program) is used that contains instructions as to what an automated system has to do.

Using sensors

Automated systems use sensors to gather data. These sensors then feed the data back to the processor that is controlling the system. The processor uses the data to vary its output.

Now you try

Copy out this table, complete it and add to it if you can.

Sensor type	*Possible use*
Gas sensor	
Heat sensor	
Light sensor	
Pressure sensor	
Radiation sensor	

Next steps

Using a control language to write control programs

A 'high-level language' called a **control language** is used to write programs with instructions to control the automated system. Control languages have special features which help design control programs. They have special commands for controlling robot movements and have special input/output facilities.

Using embedded systems

An embedded system is a computer system with its own operating system and processors embedded, usually inside a machine in order to control it. The embedded system is normally a small, single processor which has limited functions. Examples are within washing machines, video recorders, games consoles, car control systems and mobile phones. Normally the user has simple control buttons, and a touch screen or menu selection to interact with the system.
Embedded systems are based on the use of microprocessors such as the Intel Pentium M processor which is designed for low-power embedded systems.

Robo-sapiens: the intelligent robot?

A new breed of robots is being developed. They are capable of many sophisticated tasks and have their own processing power, memory and a range of different sensors and motors to help them perform their tasks. How do they differ from the industrial robots we have been looking at up to now?

- They have access to powerful processors on the robot itself.
- Some have wireless links which enable them to tap into powerful processors on servers or PCs.
- Some even have multiple networked systems. An example is a processor with real-time avoidance systems in the base to prevent collisions and another system in the 'head' to navigate and scan ahead. The two processors are then networked to coordinate the robot's actions.

What sensors do they use to give them human-like senses?

- Optical sensors are used to 'see' objects.
- Sonar beams and sensors are used to navigate, rather like a bat.

Next steps continued

- Tactile sensors are used in the base so that they can detect different types of surface they are travelling over: carpets, wooden floors etc.
- Microphones and voice recognition software is used to take in commands.

These developments mean that the intelligent robots are able to perform a wide range of tasks, from space exploration to flying planes and even household chores.

An experimental intelligent robot

Fig 3.10

Now you try

1. Write a list of machines with embedded systems in them which you have used.
2. Search the Internet for examples of intelligent robots, and write a short description of *two* of them. Include details of their sensors and their processing capabilities.

Analogue and digital signals

What kinds of sensor do automated systems use?

In an automated system, sensors feed data in the form of *analogue* signals back to the *digital* processor.

Analogue signals vary continuously. If we were to draw an analogue signal it would look like a wave as it rises and falls.

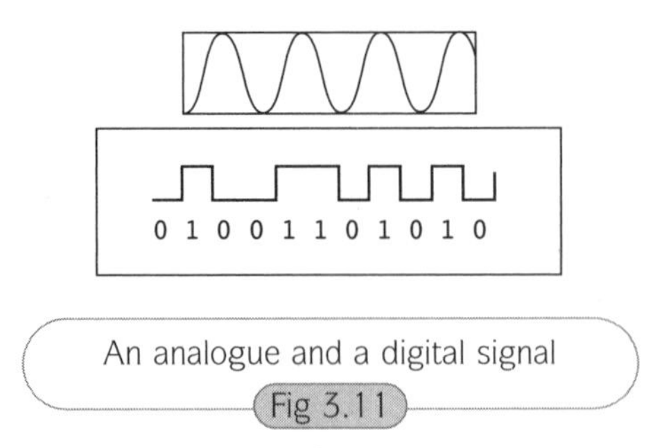

An analogue and a digital signal

Fig 3.11

A sensor detecting light sends out an analogue signal which rises and falls with the light levels. The problem is that the processor 'understands' only digital data, made up of ones and zeros (1s and 0s). The solution is to have an **interface**. An interface is needed to convert the data from analogue to digital form (Figure 3.12).

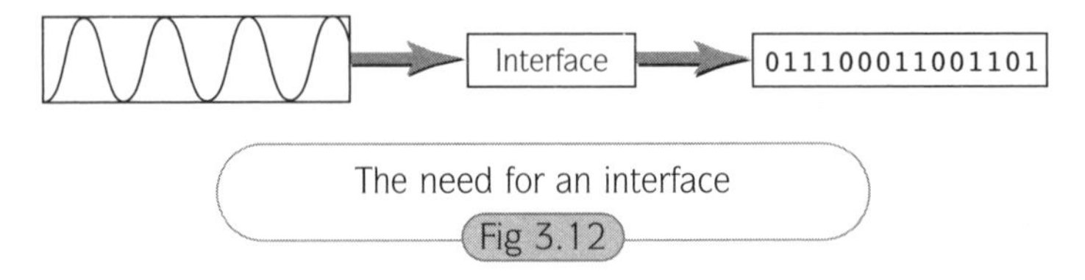

The need for an interface

Fig 3.12

Next steps

A/D convertor

An interface which changes an analogue signal to a digital form is known as an **A/D convertor**. How does it change analogue into digital? It takes thousands of *samples* of the incoming analogue signal every second and turns them into digital data (Figure 3.13).

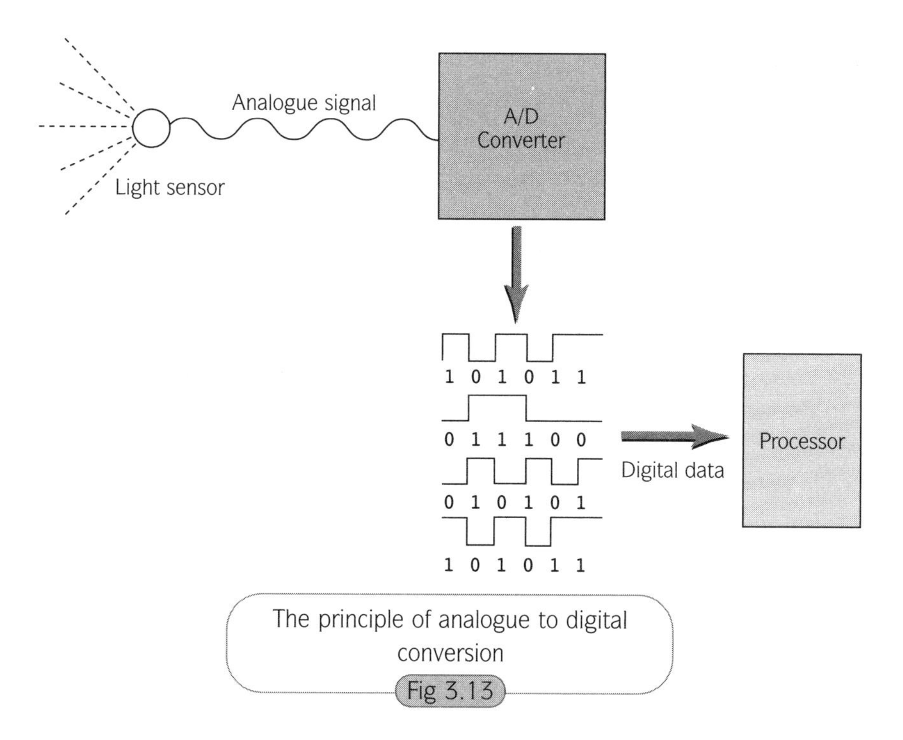

The principle of analogue to digital conversion

Fig 3.13

D/A convertor

An interface which changes digital information into analogue form is known as a **D/A convertor**. This type of convertor is used when the processor is sending signals out to control a machine or a robot arm.

Where are the convertors stored?

The software which carries out the analogue-to-digital and digital-to-analogue coversions is often stored on ROM (read-only memory) chips. This means it is instantly available to the system and there is no need for the system to be delayed while the software is loaded in from backing storage.

Real-time processing

In **real-time** processing the system reacts instantly. Take the example of a robot arm being controlled by a computer system:

- The incoming analogue signals from sensors are converted to digital form.
- The data is then processed and the system reacts instantly to control the robot arm.

Real time processing enables automated systems to react fast enough to control machinery.

Now you try

1 Why does an automated system need an interface?

Credit questions

2 What is the job of a D/A convertor on a system controlling a robot arm?

3 List the range of sensors that might be found on an intelligent robot.

4 Search the Internet for an example of an intelligent robot. Write a summary of its key features. Include a graphic if you can.

The Glasgow Science Centre Tower

The Science Centre Tower in Glasgow is a spectacular example of an automated system. The giant tower has a viewing platform which people can reach by a lift. From there you can see a panoramic view of the city of Glasgow and the surrounding countryside.
The Glasgow tower has two special features (Figure 3.14):

- It has a special streamlined shape so that it can face directly into the prevailing wind.
- It can be rotated to face into the wind.

This means that the automated system rotates the tower according to the prevailing wind speed and direction.

How it works

The tower sits on large rollers which are turned by powerful electric motors. The motors are controlled by a computerised control unit.

Sensors on two weather stations, one at the top of the tower and one near the bottom, gather information about wind speed and direction, temperature, humidity and rainfall. The data from the wind speed and direction sensors is fed to the control unit at the base of the tower by using radio modems.

The control unit then processes this data before sending control signals to the motors to adjust the position of the tower.

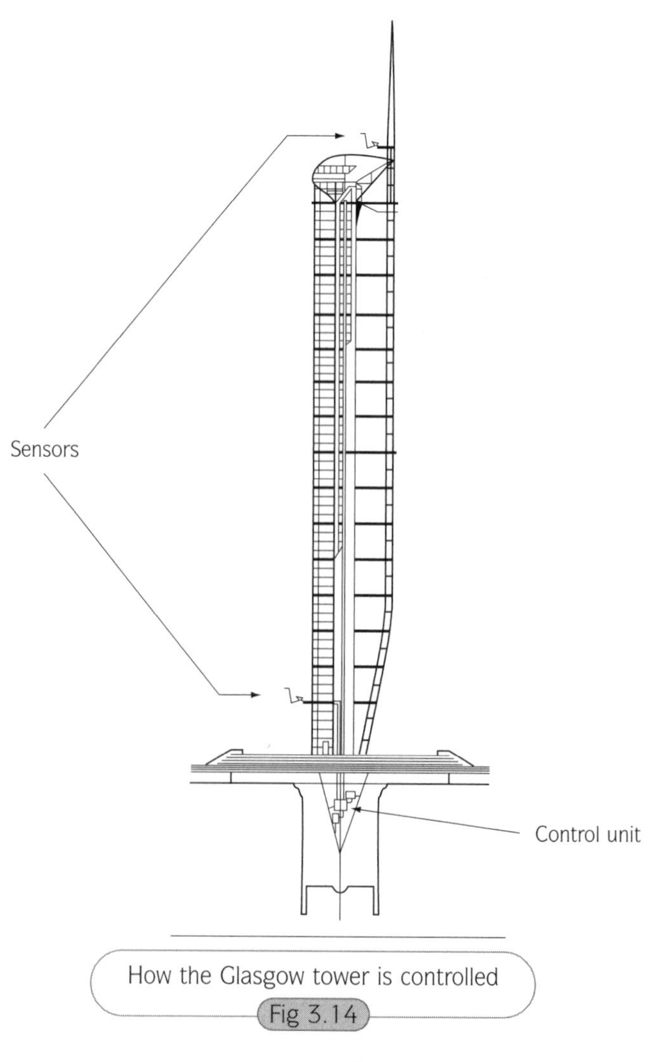

How the Glasgow tower is controlled
Fig 3.14

Now you try

1 What sensors does the Glasgow Science Centre Tower use?
2 Why is an automated system used to control the position of the tower?
3 Visit the Glasgow Science Centre's website (use a search engine) and find out about the tower for yourself.

Knowledge check 2

1 What type of language is used to write the software that controls automated systems?
2 What are sensors used for?
3 List *four* sensors that could be used by an automated system, and describe a situation in which each might be used.
4 What is the job of an interface?
5 Why does an automated system need a *real-time* system to operate effectively?
6 What is simulation and what is it used for?

Credit questions

7 Explain A/D conversion.
8 What is an embedded system?
9 What is an intelligent robot?
10 Describe the sensors an intelligent robot might have.

The economics of automated systems

The initial costs

The setting up of an automated system involves many costs:

- the cost of buying and installing a computer system
- the cost of robots
- the cost of guidance systems for mobile robots
- the cost of installing sensors
- the cost of developing the control software
- the cost of training people to operate and maintain the system.

Long-term savings

The high initial costs are soon balanced by the lower running costs, and

- an increase in the rate of production
- an increase in the quality of goods produced
- a decrease in running costs (since there are fewer workers, the wage bill is lower).

Now you try

How can the high level of initial investment in an automated system be justified?

Automated systems and people's jobs

Job creation, training and redundancy

When an automated system is introduced, existing workers need to be trained in the use of the new technology. If a mobile robot is introduced into a factory, some staff will need to be trained to operate and control the robot. Other staff will need to know how the robot affects their job: it might be delivering materials to their part of the factory.

Some jobs, such as welding in a car factory, are often completely taken over by the robots and the people made redundant.

Automated systems tend to create the following jobs:

- a *systems analyst* to design the system
- *programmers* to write and test the software
- *engineers* to install and test the system
- *engineers* to maintain the system
- *operators* to run and monitor the system.

Safety systems

When an automated system involving robots is installed, you have to think of safety. You have to make sure that people working alongside an automated system are not injured by robot arms, mobile robots or other computer-controlled machinery.

One safety measure is to mark out the areas where automated systems are operating by:

- painting hatched areas on the floor in bright yellow
- erecting overhead signs.

Mobile robots can be fitted with flashing lights and sirens. Pressure sensors can be fitted to mobile robots to detect when they come into contact with objects.

Now you try

1. Some people are worried about the effect on jobs of introducing automated systems. Write out a list of things you could say to reassure them.
2. Other people are worried about the danger to people's safety which stationary and mobile robots bring. Again, what could you say to reassure them?

Next steps

Effects on the design of a workplace

Installing an automated system can mean completely redesigning a workplace.

Think of the things that need to be done to have a mobile robot system installed in a factory. The following would need to be installed (Figure 3.15):

- sensors
- a guidance system
- power cables and data cables
- a controlling computer system
- safety systems.

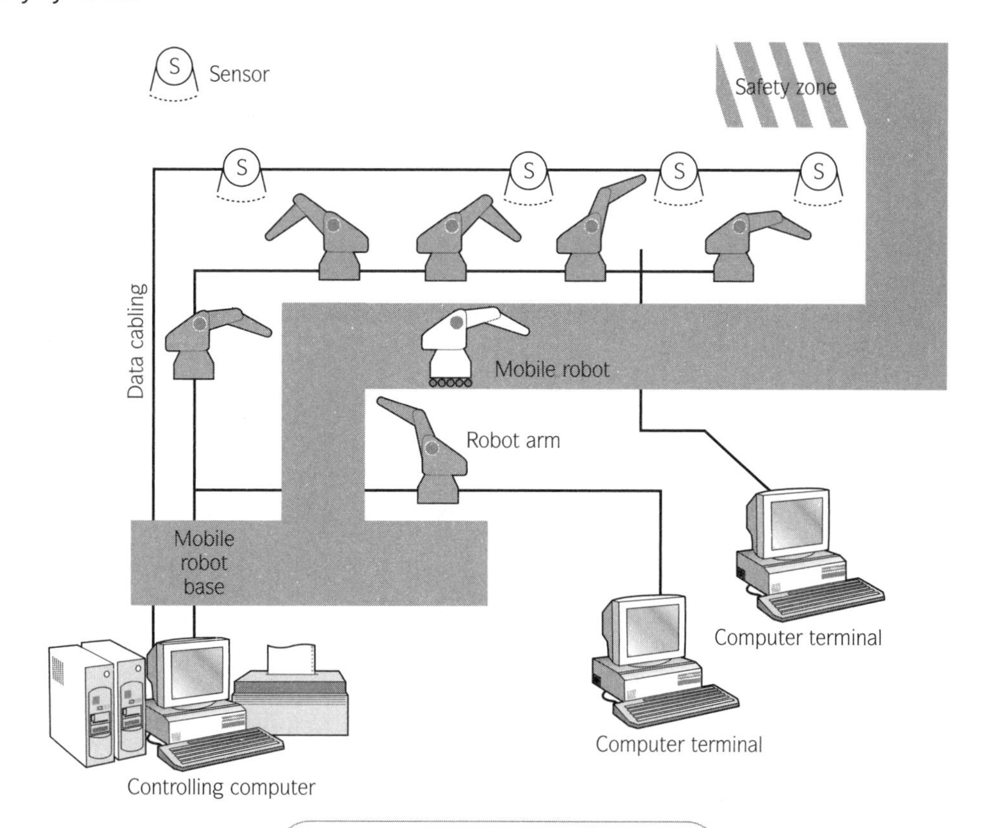

A workplace with a mixture of mobile and stationary robots needs to be safe

Fig 3.15

Knowledge check 3

1. Why are the intial costs of an automated system so high?
2. Give an example of each of the following: (a) initial costs; and (b) running costs.
3. How do automated systems reduce costs in the long term?
4. What safety measures could be taken to make mobile robots safe to work alongside?
5. What jobs does an automated system create?

Credit questions

6. Describe the job of a systems analyst in setting up a factory equipped with robots.
7. How would the introduction of mobile robots affect the design of a factory floor?

End of unit progress check

Questions

1 Complete the passage below:
Reasons for using automated systems:
They can operate in ______ places.
When they do a job they are very ______ .
They can do repetitive jobs without making ______ . 3

2 List *three* tools you might find fitted to a robot arm. 3

3 Label the robot arm below correctly. 2

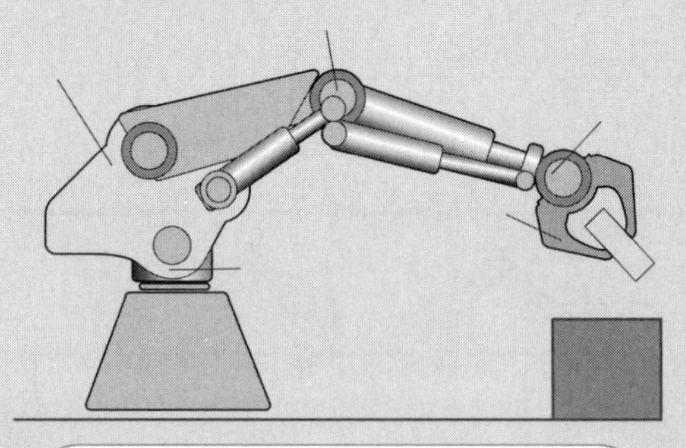

What are the parts of this stationary robot arm called?

Fig 3.16

4 A car factory needs to have some mobile robots installed.

(a) What type of guidance system would you recommend? 1

(b) Explain how it works. 2

(c) Give a reason for choosing that guidance system. 1

5 The car factory managers decide that it is taking far too long to design and make their new models. One of them suggests using a CAD/CAM system. Give *two* reasons why this is a good suggestion. 2

6 Copy and complete the following chart. Use these words;
real time processing, virtual reality, sensors, simulation, high level instructions

This could be used for training an airline pilot	
An architect could use this to check out the details of the inside of a building he/she has designed	
Automated systems are controlled by programs containing . . .	
A robot arm needs this to react quickly and do its work	
These are needed to feed information back to the processor	

5

7 What is the job of an interface? 1

8 A mobile robot causes a few accidents in the factory. Describe *two* safety measures that could be taken to prevent more accidents. 2

Foundation/general total 22 marks

Credit questions

9 Describe how an A/D convertor works. 2

10 A factory has to be redesigned because it is being fitted with mobile and stationary robots. Describe *three* key aspects of the new layout which the *systems analyst* will have to consider. 3

11 An important advantage of automated systems is that they are adaptable. Explain what this means. 3

12 Describe the ways in which an intelligent robot is different from a robot arm in a factory. 2

Credit total 10 marks

Computer systems

What you will read about in this unit

- Languages and translators
- Operating systems
- Low-level machine
- Hardware
  - Backing storage
  - Input devices
  - Output devices

Languages and translators

We are going to look at the languages used to write computer programs, and then the translators used to turn the programs into **machine code**.

Machine code is the only language that a computer really understands. It is made of binary numbers like this: 01101100. Machine code is difficult to read and write. Imagine having to write all your programs using machine code – it would be really difficult. We use **high-level languages** instead.

High-level languages

Examples of high-level languages are Truebasic, Visual Basic, Pascal, Cobol, Fortran and C++. Such languages are made up of instructions that look very like English. This makes them easier to write and to edit. They are also *portable*, which means that they can be transferred from one machine to another. They can be written on one computer system and then transferred to and run on other systems.

Now you try

- Which high-level language do you use for your programs?
- Write out a few lines of coding in your high-level language. Do you think it is similar to English?

Translators

Remember, at the lowest level the system understands only machine code, like this:

01101100 01110001 01111000 1111110 000101 01111010 1110101 10101010
01010101 11100011 00011101 00011111 11100010 10101111 01011111 10101100
00110011 11001100 10101010 01100110 11110000 11101100 01110001 01111000
1111110 000101 01111010 1110101 10101010 01010101 11100011 00011101
00011111 11100010 10101111 01011111 10101100 00110011 11001100 10101010

All programs written in a high-level language need to be translated into machine code before they can be run by the system (Figure 4.1).

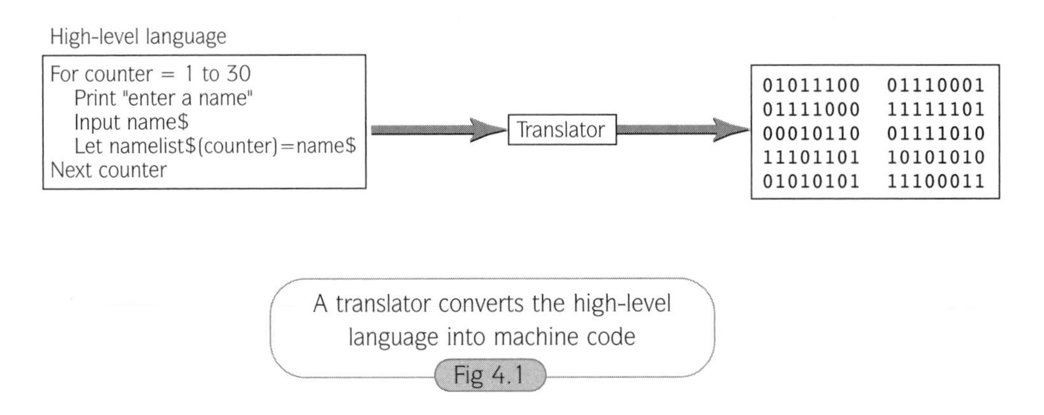

A translator converts the high-level language into machine code

Fig 4.1

There are different types of translator, each with its own advantages and disadvantages.

Next steps

Interpreters

Interpreters translate one instruction at a time from a high-level language into machine code *every time the program is run*. This is a slow process but it is very useful when trying to find errors in a program. The advantage of an interpreter is that it gives an error message straight away when the program is run. This is a great help when learning to write programs since errors can be detected and corrected immediately.

A disadvantage of using an interpreter is that since each line is translated into machine code each time the program is run, an interpreted program is slower to run than a compiled program. For example, an interpreter would translate this loop 30 times every time it runs the program:

```
For counter = 1 to 30
   Print 'enter a name'
   Input name$
   Let namelist$(counter)=name$
Next counter
```

Compilers

A compiler translates high-level language instructions (the **source code**) into machine code (the **object code**). Once it has done the translation it saves the machine code version, the object code.

A compiler has the advantage that it translates the high-level language instructions only *once*. It then stores the machine code for future use. This means that compiled programs are much faster than interpreted programs.

One disadvantage is that a compiler translates all the high-level language instructions at the one time after they have been keyed in. This means that many errors are not spotted until the programmer has finished. This can be a bit awkward when you are learning to program using a compiled language.

Next steps continued

Portability

High level languages are **portable**. This means they can be written on one computer system and then transferred to and run on other systems. Programs written in assembly language are low level, specific to one type of processor, and are not portable.

Now you try

1. What kind of translator do you use when you translate your high-level language coding?
2. Does your translator give error messages as you enter the coding or at the end when you have finished writing your program and you ask for it to be translated?
3. How can you prove that your program is portable?

Knowledge check 1

1 What is machine code?

2 Complete these sentences:

(a) A high-level language is very like _______.

(b) A high-level language helps you write programs to _____ _______.

Credit questions

3 Match up the translators with the descriptions:

	It translates each line one at a time every time the program runs.
	It translates the high-level language into machine code once only.
	It points out the syntax errors as you write the program.
	Using this translator your program, written in a high-level language, runs faster because it is only translated once and then the machine code is saved.
	This translator shows you your errors after you have entered all your coding in a high-level language, when you try to translate the program.

Operating systems

An operating system is a program that controls all the tasks your computer does for you. What sort of jobs does it do?

- It reads in data from your keyboard and mouse.
- It sends data to your printer.
- It sends text and graphics to your screen.
- It loads data into the memory from the hard drive.
- It saves files to your disk.

File types

Data files

These contain the information needed by a program in order to run. Figure 4.2 shows the contents of a directory containing database, spreadsheet and word processing data files.

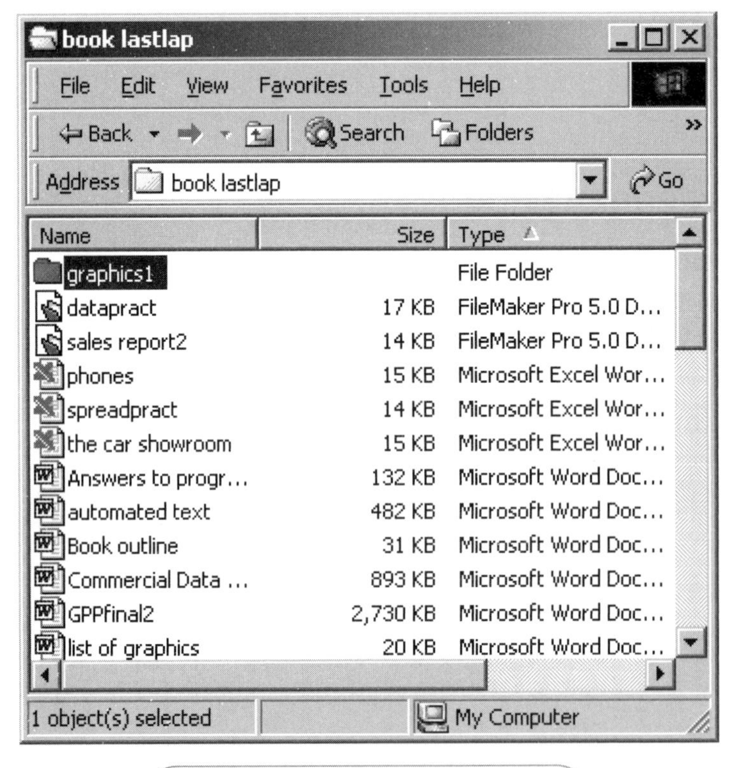

The contents of a directory

Fig 4.2

Program files

These contain the instructions that make up the software which the system will run. Figure 4.3 shows all the directories holding the program files.

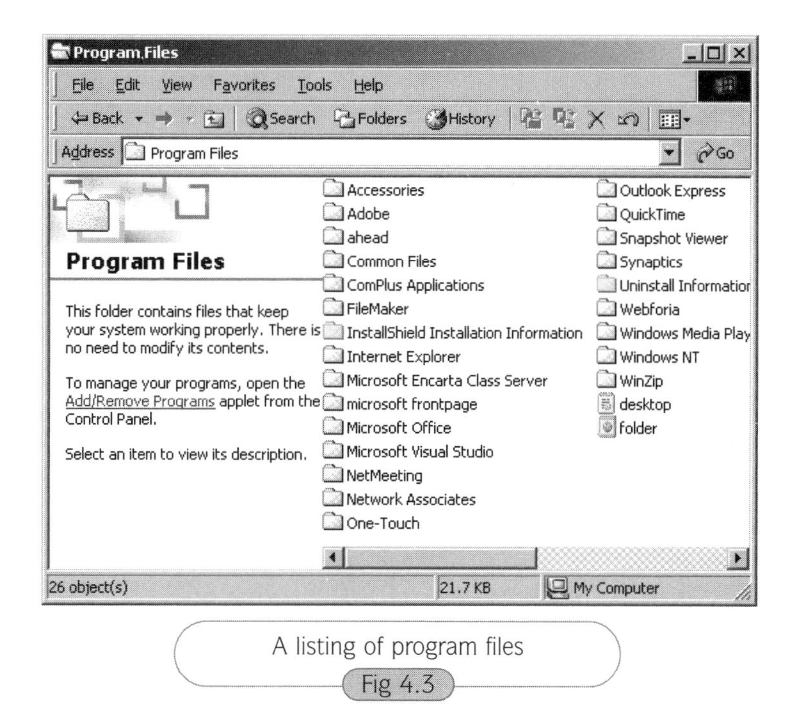

A listing of program files

Fig 4.3

Now you try

1 Open up the window of the directory (folder) that holds your word processing files. Are these data files or program files? Explain your answer.
2 Have a look through your computer's desktop and see whether you can tell the difference between a program file and a data file by looking at the icons.
3 List the jobs that the operating system carries out when you click on one of your word processing file icons.

Next steps

The HCI

The operating system provides the human–computer interface (HCI) for the user. The most common HCIs are based on the use of graphics, windows, icons and pull-down menus.
When a user wants the computer to save a file or load a file from a disk, all that it is necessary to do is click on an icon or select from a menu using a pointer. To load the paint program in the illustration (Figure 4.4), all the user has to do is open the menu and click the mouse.

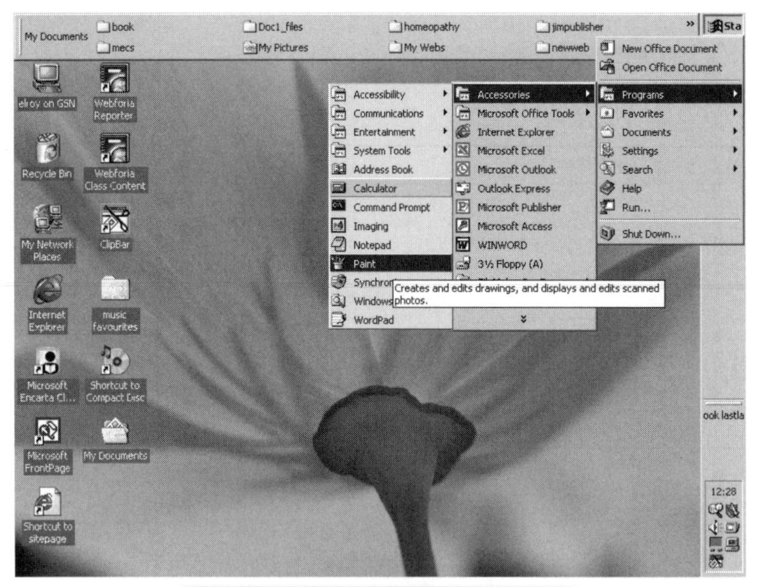

The Desktop and the Start menu in the MS operating system

Fig 4.4

The operating system checks the movements of the mouse and pointer and translates them into instructions for the system to carry out. For example, it would:

- detect that the mouse button was clicked while the pointer was on the *paint application* on the *accessories menu*
- then issue instructions for that software to be loaded into memory from the hard disc.

File and memory management

The **file management** part of the operating system enables the user to create files and store them on disk, to store them in directories, and to control access to files. The HCI makes this an easy matter of manipulating the file and folder icons.

The **memory management** part of the operating system loads files into the computer's memory. Again the HCI makes this easy for the user.

Error reporting

When something goes wrong, for example a file can't be opened, the operating system will inform the user by displaying an error report. The HCI will present a clear, understandable message on the screen.

Device drivers

These are programs that work alongside the operating system. They help the computer work with peripherals like the printer, disc drive or the CD-writer. Each peripheral has different characteristics. For example, they work at different speeds and use different control codes and signals.

The device drivers deal with all of that, freeing the operating system from the need to understand and support the different peripherals.

Types of operating system

Interactive systems

In an interactive system the computer reacts to user requests *immediately* and processes the necessary data.

For example, in a travel agency the operator books your holiday as soon as you ask for the booking (and pay a deposit). The job is not put into a batch and processed later, but is carried out by the operating system immediately.

Real-time systems

A real time system is an operating system which works even faster than an interactive system. It is designed to process a large number of signals/operations in a very short time.

Examples of the use of real-time systems are:

- guidance systems for rockets/spacecraft and aeroplanes
- monitoring equipment in a chemical plant
- controlling machinery in a factory.

Some real-time systems have sensors attached to them and react *instantly* to information fed to them. A real-time system monitoring a petrol refinery will *instantly* set off alarms and shut down valves when its sensors detect an escape of gas or a sudden rise in temperature.

Next steps

An interactive system with background job capability

Some systems have the ability to handle both interactive enquiries and to carry out batch processing in the background. For example, in a bank the computer will be able to handle customer requests for data on account balances *interactively*. When it can find a suitable gap between interactive requests, the computer will go on to process a background task such as processing account statements.

Now you try

1 What is the key feature of an interactive system?

2 Which types of system would be most suitable for the computer (a) in a theatre booking office, and (b) controlling a robot?

Credit questions

3 Find out how a mail-order company would use an interactive system with background job capability.

Organising files

If you don't organise your files, your desktop will end up cluttered with dozens of file icons. You might get away with that if you only had a few files, but when you have lots of files it becomes difficult to find what you are looking for. So, you have to organise them into **directories.** Desktops running the Windows operating system use the term **folder** instead of directory.

You might have a directory for your programming files and another for your graphic files.

Next steps

Hierarchical structure

When you start to build up lots of directories you can arrange them in a **hierarchical structure**. This simply means that you store directories one inside another in, hopefully, a logical order. This gives you a structure with different levels. When you look at a diagram of the directory structure you can see the different levels clearly. Figure 4.5 is an example.

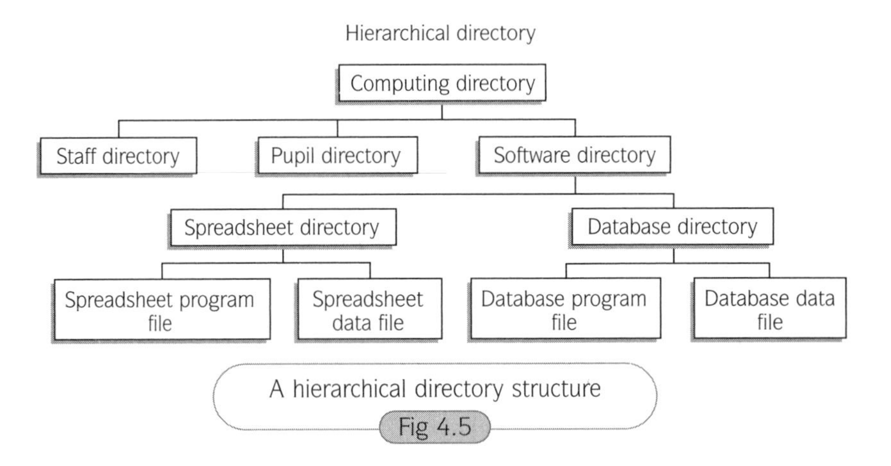

A hierarchical directory structure

Fig 4.5

A hierarchical structure is logical and orderly, making it easier to find files. It also enables you to control access to folders.

Now you try

1. Do some housekeeping on your computer system. Organise your data files into directories (folders). You should have a folder for each of the following: word processing files, spreadsheet files, database files, graphics files and programming files. You might even create some sub-directories by dividing your word processing files up into, say, *project reports* and *programming documentation*.
2. When you have organised your *directory structure*, experiment with it. Try looking for files. You should find it easier to locate the files you want to open.

Accessing files

Let us look at two ways in which the system accesses data.

Sequential access to data

In a system with **sequential access**, the system starts at the beginning of the sequence and reads each piece of data until it locates what it needs.

Consider, for example, a database file stored on magnetic tape (Figure 4.6). If the system wants to read record 6 it has to start at the beginning at record 1 and access each record in turn until it reaches the one it wants.

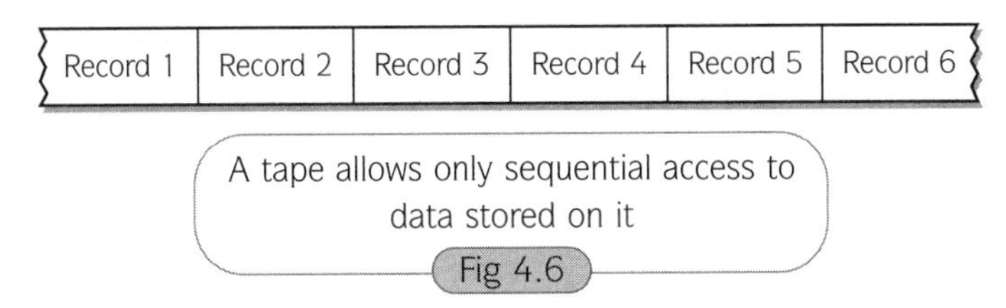

A tape allows only sequential access to data stored on it

Fig 4.6

With magnetic tape the computer uses sequential access since it starts at the beginning and reads each record in turn as the tape winds forward.

Random/direct access to data

This means the system accesses the data it needs by going directly to where it is stored (Figure 4.7). Hard disks are random-access devices, so are CD-ROMs.

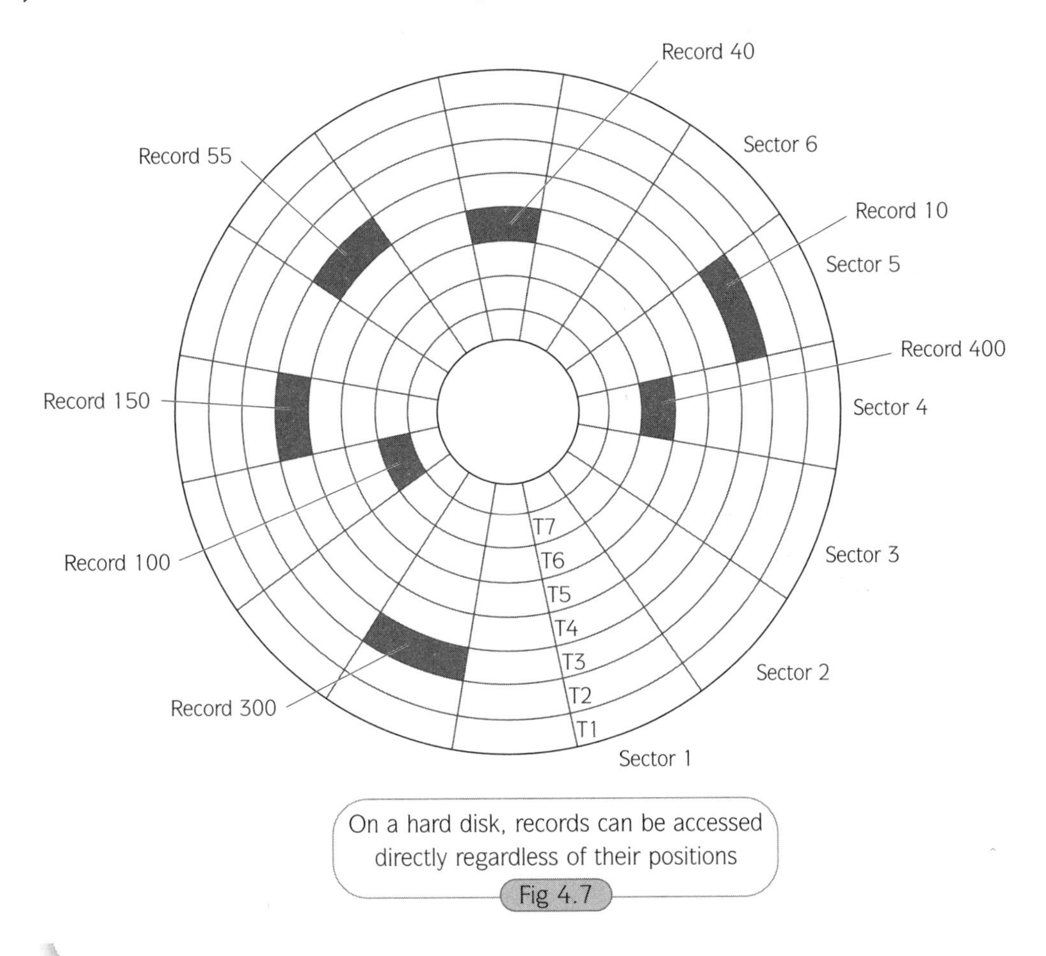

On a hard disk, records can be accessed directly regardless of their positions

Fig 4.7

Next steps continued

Random/direct access is often found in interactive systems, such as one designed to book train tickets or seats on a plane. It allows instant access to the data, unlike sequential access which takes time to go through all the data in the sequence.

Knowledge check 2

1 What is an operating system?
2 List *two* program files and *two* data files that are on your computer system.
3 What is a directory or folder used for?
4 How does an interactive system differ from a real-time system?
5 Which type of system would be suitable for: (a) booking seats on a train; (b) controlling a robot; and (c) ordering a book on the Internet?

Credit questions

6 Write down an example of an interactive system with background processing capability.
7 What is the key feature of a hierarchical directory structure?
8 List *two* advantages of using a hierarchical directory structure.
9 Describe how sequential access works.
10 Why is magnetic tape ideally suited to sequential access?
11 How does random/direct access differ from sequential access?
12 Name *two* types of backing storage that use random/direct access.

Low-level machine

This section looks at how a computer's memory and central processor work.

A computer's memory

Computers use (a) backing storage to store data and (b) main memory. There are two types of backing storage, magnetic and optical.

Main memory

Inside the computer is the main memory which is made up of memory chips. Main memory is divided into two parts: RAM and ROM.

RAM stands for 'random-access memory'. When you type in data at the keyboard, the data goes into the RAM. All data is lost when the computer is switched off. If you want to retain the data that is in RAM you have to save it to disk or to a writable CD before you switch off the power.

ROM stands for 'read-only memory'. Data stored in ROM can be read only – you cannot change it and it is not wiped out when the computer is switched off. It is available when the computer is switched on again and does not have to be loaded in from disk.

Measuring a computer's memory

We need to be able to measure the size of any backing storage and the main memory. The following terms are used:

Bit	Binary digit: a 1 or 0
Byte	8 bits e.g. 01101100
Kilobyte	1024 bytes
Megabyte	1024 kilobytes
Gigabyte	1024 megabytes
Terabyte	1024 gigabytes

Now you try

1. How much data can your hard disk hold?
2. How much data can the most modern hard disks hold? Check the latest magazines or the Internet.
3. How many megabytes of main memory does your computer have?
4. What is the size of main memory in the most modern computers? Again, check magazines or the Internet.

The processor

This is the brains of the computer (Figure 4.8). It organises the computer as it *inputs*, *processes* and *outputs* data. It takes in the data being input to the computer, processes it and then outputs it to screen or printer. Table 4.1 shows some examples.

A processor
Fig 4.8

Table 4.1 Examples of actions of the processor

Input	*Process*	*Output*
Names and addresses entered into a database	Sort them in alphabetical order	Send names and addresses to a printer
Enter a graphic using a graphics tablet	Rotate the graphic	Display the graphic on a monitor screen
Read data in from a bar code	Add cost of item to a bill	Print out total bill

Next steps

Central processing unit (CPU)

Processor structure

The processor (CPU) is made up of a **control unit** (the CU), an **arithmetic and logic unit** (the ALU), and **registers**.

The control unit issues control signals to organise:

- the storing of data in memory
- the fetching of data from memory
- the carrying out of instructions.

The arithmetic and logic unit carries out the arithmetic and logical functions. Arithmetic functions include addition, subtraction, multiplication and division. One example of a logic function is comparing values. The processor carries out a logic operation when it processes the following instructions:

```
While score >100 or score <0
  print "Out of range. Please re-enter"
  input score
End while
```

Here the ALU *compares* the value held in the variables *score* with the numbers 100 and 0. If either of these comparisons is true then the out-of-range message is displayed.

Registers

Registers are memory locations on the actual processor. It uses them to store data, instructions and memory addresses.

Word power

A *word* is the amount of data that the processor can move in and out of memory and manipulate at any one time. The size of the word helps you measure the power of your system.

- If a computer has a 16-bit word it can manipulate16 bits at a time.
- If a computer has a 32-bit word it can manipulate 32 bits at a time.

Memory addresses

The computer's main memory is divided up into locations. Each location has an *address* and each one can store data. In Figure 4.9, each location holds 32 bits of data.

Next steps continued

Location address | Contents

Location address	Contents
011110101001110	11110000101010101010101001010101
011110011110101	01010101111111110101010110101011
011110101001100	11110000101010101010101101010101
011110011010101	01010101111001110101010110101011

In this example each location holds 32 bits of data

A computer's main memory is divided into locations with addresses

Fig 4.9

When the main processor is retrieving data from memory it uses the address to find the data.

Knowledge check 3

1 The processor is the ______________.

2 The processor organises the i____, p______, and o_____.

3 Complete these sentences:

(a) You cannot store data in ROM because it is ____ ____.

(b) When you type in data at the keyboard it is stored in RAM, but when you switch off __ __ ______.

4 Copy and complete the following table:

8 bits	_ byte
1024 megabytes	_ byte
1024 bytes	_ byte
1024 kilobytes	_ byte
1024 gigabytes	_ byte

Credit question

5 Copy out the table, then complete it by choosing the correct match from the list below:

	The processor uses this to store data, instructions and addresses
	These are the two parts of the processor
	Each of these has its own address
	This sends out signals to fetch instructions and carry them out
	This is an example of a *logic* operation

register, comparing two values, control unit, address, arithmetic and logic unit/control unit

How computers store numbers, text and graphics

Storing numbers

As humans we use decimal numbers to represent quantities: 0, 1, 2, 3, 4, 5, 6, 7, 8, 9 etc. In contrast, computers use *binary numbers*. For example, in the binary numbering system 10000001 represents the equivalent of 65 in decimal numbering. Computers change our decimal numbers into binary numbers before doing anything with them.

Binary numbers

Binary numbers go up in powers of 2 and can be used to represent any decimal number. Have a careful look at Figure 4.10. Using the table it is easy to see how the binary number 1000001 equals the decimal number 64 + 1, which is 65.

2^7	2^6	2^5	2^4	2^3	2^2	2^1	2^0	Power of 2
128	64	32	16	8	4	2	1	Decimal
0	1	0	0	0	0	0	1	Binary
	=64			+			1	=65

The relationship between binary and decimal numbers

Fig 4.10

Using binary numbers in this simple way, the computer can easily represent, store and manipulate any whole number.

Now you try

Write out the binary numbers for 64, 65, 66, 67, 68 and 69.

Knowledge check 4

1 Computers use _____ numbers. The numbers are made up of ones and _____.

Credit questions

2 Complete the following table:

1000001 =	65
1000010 =	
1000011 =	
1000100 =	

3 Copy out and complete the following table. Then work out what the binary number is in decimal.

2	2^6	2^5	2^4	2^3	2^2	2^1	2^0	Power of 2
	64	32	16	8	4	2	1	Decimal
0		0	1	0	1	0	1	Binary

Storing text

A computer stores text by using a code. The most common code is ASCII, which stands for **A**merican **S**tandard **C**ode for **I**nformation **I**nterchange.

Each character in the ASCII code is represented by its own unique binary number. Table 4.2 shows examples of some of the code.

Table 4.2 Common examples of the ASCII code

Binary	*Decimal*	*Representing*
1000001	65	A
1000010	66	B
1000011	67	C
1000100	68	D
1000101	69	E
1000110	70	F

Now you try

Write out your name in letters and then put it into the ASCII code using either decimal or binary numbers.

Storing graphics

A graphic can be a drawing, a graph, a painting or a photograph. A computer stores graphics by using binary code to represent **pixels**. A pixel is a point on the screen (Figure 4.11).

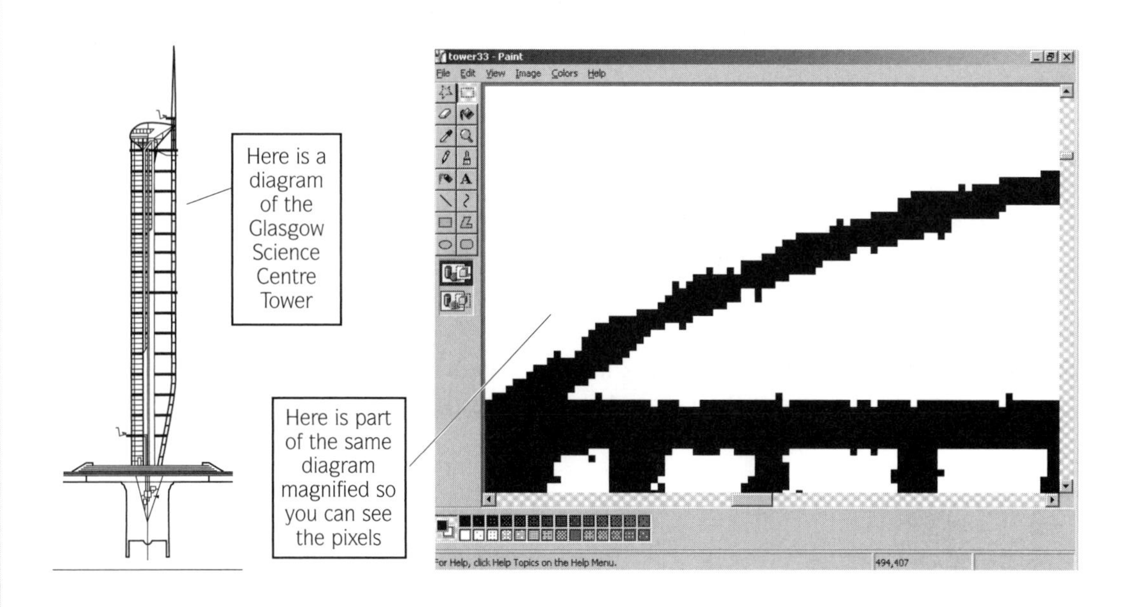

Each point on the screen is a pixel

Fig 4.11

In a simple black and white graphic, the pattern of filled and blank pixels can be represented by patterns of binary numbers (Figure 4.12). Each square or pixel filled in is represented by a 1, while each square or pixel left blank is represented by a 0.

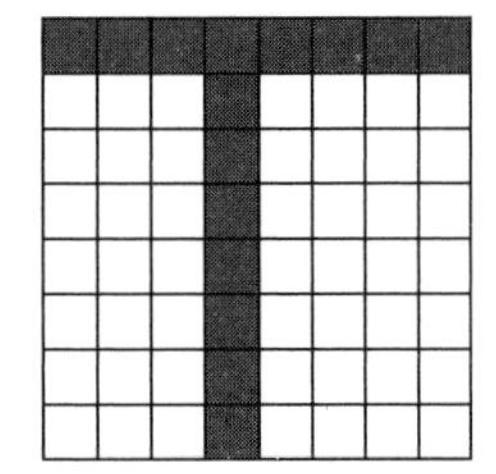

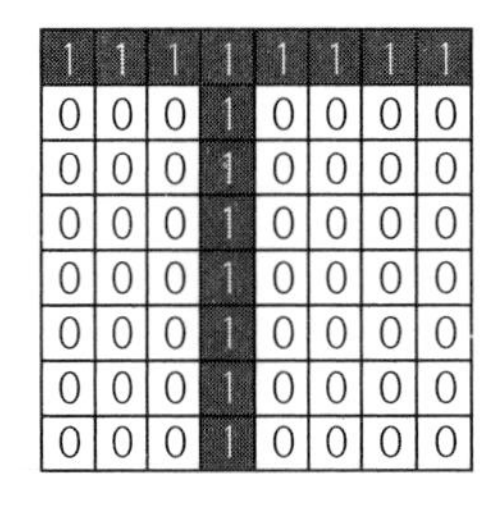

A simple black and white graphic can be represented by a pattern of binary numbers

Fig 4.12

If a pixel is coloured it needs more than one binary number to represent it. If you have your computer set up to display 256 colours, it will need to have 8 bits for each pixel, because 256 is equal to 2^8.

Next steps

Calculating the storage space for black and white graphics

Look at the graphic in Figure 4.12. How do you find out how much storage space will be needed to store this graphic?

- The graphic has 8 bits across and 8 bits down.
- Multiply them together and you get 8 times 8 = 64 bits.
- You can then turn this into bytes by dividing by 8. So 64 bits divided by 8 equals 8 bytes.

Here is another example. What if the graphic was 8 bits across and 16 bits down?

- The total number of bits would be: 8 times 16 = 128 bits.
- You can then turn this into bytes by dividing by 8. So 128 bits divided by 8 equals 16 bytes.

Now you try

1 Draw a 16 × 16 grid and shade in a simple shape. Then write out the binary pattern for that shape.
2 Calculate how much storage space your simple graphic would need.
3 How much storage space would a 2 inch by 2 inch black and white graphic need when stored at 300 dots per inch?

Knowledge check 5

1. ASCII stands for A_______ S_______ C___ for I__________ I__________.
2. The ASCII code gives each number, letter and punctuation mark its own unique ______ ______.
3. Work out the decimal equivalents of the following binary numbers: (a) 01000001, (b) 1000010, and (c) 1000011.
4. Copy and complete the table.

A point on the screen is a	
In a black and white drawing each pixel is represented by	
The storage needed for a black and white graphic 8 pixels × 8 pixels is	

Backing storage

Storage is made up of a range of devices which the computer has access to. Your computer will have one or more of the following types: a floppy disk drive, a hard disk, a CD-ROM drive, a re-writable CD drive, and posssibly a tape drive.

Magnetic storage

Floppy disks

These are made from circular plastic plates coated in ferric oxide. Data is stored on the surface as patterns of magnetic spots. The advantages of this are:

- data can be accessed directly
- the disks are cheap
- the disks are compact and easy to handle and store.

However, these disks have limited storage capacity: a high-density disk (HDD) can hold just 1.44 megabytes of data. The disks can also be damaged easily by dust, dampness, or stray electromagnetic pulses.

Hard disks

A hard disk drive contains several rigid metal disks. The surfaces of these disks are divided into *tracks* and *sectors* on which data is stored as patterns of magnetic spots. The drive is sealed to prevent dust corrupting the data, and is usually fixed inside the computer (some can be removed). Figure 4.13 shows the inside of a typical hard disk drive.

The *read/write heads*, suspended a fraction above the disk surfaces, can access data very quickly since the disks spin at high speed (typically 7–10,000 rpm).

Modern hard disk drives have high storage capacity, which means they can hold gigabytes of data. They enable direct and random access to data stored on the disk surfaces.

The inside of a hard disk

Fig 4.13

Tape storage

Tapes can be used as a form of backing storage (see Figure 4.14). Tapes kept on cartridges or reels store data in binary using magnetic spots to encode the data. Key features of tapes as a form of backing storage are:

- they have a large capacity
- they have fast data transfer rates – up to 30 megabytes per second
- they are ideally suited for data that is stored and accessed sequentially.

Information on tapes degrades eventually, so they are best suited to medium- and short-term storage needs. Tapes need to be stored in a suitably controlled environment as they are vulnerable to changes in temperature, to humidity and to dust.

DAT tapes holding up to 200 gigabytes are used for backing up data.

A tape drive

Fig 4.14

Knowledge check 6

1. List the *three* types of magnetic backing storage.
2. Copy and complete the following table:

This holds 1.44 Mbytes	
In modern PCs these hold 100+ gigabytes	
One of these cartridges can hold up to 200 gigabytes	

3. Copy and complete the following table:

They are useful when transferring small files to another computer	
They are used as the main backing storage on most computers	
They are used to make backups	
They are usually sealed inside your computer to keep them free from dust	
They are very cheap and cost only a few pence	

Optical storage

CD-ROMs

Compact disc read-only memory is an optical form of storing data. That means it uses *laser optics* technology to store and read the data. Data is stored in binary form by using lasers to burn microscopic marks on the disc's surface. The binary patterns are then read by a sensor which detects light reflected from the surface.

The discs are direct-access devices. They are also read-only devices and so are not suitable for storing data that needs to be updated regularly.

CD-ROMs have very high capacity: a standard disc can hold 650 megabytes.

DVDs

Like a CD-ROM, a DVD uses laser technology to store and read data. Like a CD-ROM it is read-only. DVDs use narrower laser beams to read and write the data on to the disk. This means they can store much more data than a CD-ROM.

An ordinary DVD can hold 4.7 gigabytes of data. A double-sided, multi-layered DVD can store up to 17 gigabytes. This means they can store very large files such as those needed to store a movie. Movies are compressed and then stored on a DVD.

CD-Rs

CD-R stands for 'compact disc recordable'. Each disc has a layer of dye. Using a laser the CD-writer creates patterns of 'spots' on the dye. These patterns of spots are used to encode and store binary data.

Once you have written a file to a CD-R you cannot delete the file or amend it, as you can on a hard disk. Once it is written to it works just like a CD-ROM. It is read-only.

CD-RWs

CD-RW stands for 'compact disc re-writable, and unlike a CD-R, you can write to them again and again'. A CD-writer uses a laser to write data to the disc. The laser is used to change the reflective properties of the disk surface to represent patterns of binary numbers.

CD-RWs are used for:

- backing up large files
- storing large multimedia presentations
- storing large programs, including games software.

Optical disc drives are slower to access than hard disks. However, they have the advantage that they are removeable. That means you can take them out of the drive and store them on a rack or shelf.

DVD-Rs

These are DVD disks that you can write to. What is the difference between them and a CD-R? It is simply that they can store more data. A DVD-R can store up to 4.7 gigabytes.

DVD-R/Ws

These are DVD disks that you can write to time and time again. They use the same laser technology as CD-RW to change the reflective properties of the disk surface in order to represent binary numbers. Their advantage over CD-RW is that they can hold much more data: a single-sided single-layer DVD can hold up to 4.7 gigabytes.

Now you try

1 Find out the capacity of the hard disk on your computer at school.
2 Find out how backups are made of the data on your school's computers. If tapes are used, how much data can they hold?
3 What CD-ROMs do you use in school? Is there any advantage in having this data on the CD-ROM?
4 Do you have access to a re-writable CD drive? If so, what is it mainly used for? What do you notice about its speeds?
5 What are DVD-ROMs often used for?

USB flash drive

This is an erasable, re-writable memory chip that holds its data when the power is switched off, or when it is removed from the computer system.

It is used as a type of backup and can be easily plugged into a PC using the USB port.

Flash drives vary in capacity from 64 Mbytes to 128 Mbytes. Being the size of a marker pen they are very easy to carry about in your pocket, or even attach to your key ring.

A USB flash drive

Fig 4.15

Knowledge check 7

1 Complete the following, using the words and phrases:
reflecting light from the surface, CD-R, CD-ROM,CD-RW, 650 Mbytes.

(a) You can't write any data to a ______.
(b) You can store a lot of information on a CD-ROM because it holds ___ ______ of data.
(c) The computer reads the data by __________ _____ ____ ___ _______ of the disc.
(d) A ____ would be suitable for storing a large computer game.
(e) The data stored on a _____ could be changed if necessary.
(f) A ______ could be useful for storing and distributing large multimedia presentations.

2 Are these statements about USB flash drives true or false?

Statement	*True/false*
A USB flash drive is a memory chip	
You can store data on it and then change it	
You can unplug it from the computer and put it in your pocket	
It holds the same amount of data as a floppy disc	
When you unplug it from the computer it loses data	

3 You have developed a website. Complete with graphics it is around 98 Mbytes in size, and you want to transfer a copy of all the files to your friend's computer. Which type of removeable backing storage would be most suitable – a floppy disc, a USB stick, a CD-ROM? Give reasons for your answer.

Now you try

Comparing backup storage

You are going to be set a task which involves comparing all the different types of backing storage according to their capacity, speed of data transfer and cost. Make sure you fill in your chart using the latest examples of the various forms of backing storage.

Table 4.3 will help you, but you must remember that the technology changes so quickly that the figures given may well be out of date. There are no costs entered on the chart because they change so quickly. *Search on the Internet or read an up-to-date computer magazine to get the latest information.*

Table 4.3

Type of backing storage	*Name and model*	*capacity*	*Speed of data transfer*
Floppy		1.44 Mbytes	Slow
Hard disk	Samsung Spinpoint sp1604n	160 Gbytes	92.6 Mbytes/s
USB stick	Iomega mini-drive	63, 128 or 256 Mbytes	1Mbyte/s
CD-ROM		600 Mbytes	The speed of CD drives varies greatly The speed is given as a number e.g. 32X 1X = 150 Kbytes/s CD-ROMs have one speed: a **reading** speed
CD-R		700 Mbytes	This will have two speeds, one for **writing** data and one for **reading** data E.g. **writing 16X** and **reading 32X**
CD-RW		700 Mbytes	This will have three speeds, one for **writing** data, one for **re-writing** and one for **reading** E.g. **writing 32X**, **re-writing 12X** and **reading 32X**
DVD-ROM		Up to 17 Gbytes	DVD disk speeds are different from CD speeds 1X for a DVD disk = 1250 Kbytes/s DVD-ROMs will have one speed for **reading**
DVD-RW		4.7 Gbytes	This will have three speeds, one for **writing**, one for **re-writing** and one for **reading** data E.g. **writing 4X**, **re-writing 2.4X** and **reading 12X**

Now copy and complete the following table using the most up-to-date information you can find using the Internet or a computing magazine.

Type of backing storage	*Name and model*	*Capacity*	*Speed of data transfer*	*Cost*

Input devices

Mouse and trackball

You use a mouse to control your pointer, to select icons and to make choices from the menus. A trackball is similar to a mouse except that the ball and buttons are both on the top (Figure 4.16). The trackball does not move. Instead, to move the cursor, you move the ball.

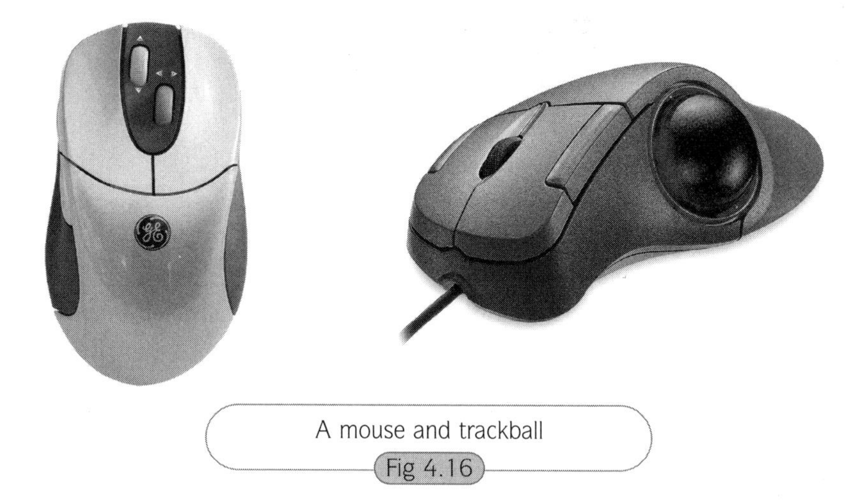

A mouse and trackball

Fig 4.16

Trackpad

This is a small pad which senses the movement of your finger and lets you control the position of the pointer on the screen by moving your finger across the pad. If you were using a mouse you would select an icon by clicking. With a trackpad you select by tapping your finger on the pad.

Graphics tablet

A graphics tablet is a flat plastic pad with electronic sensors below the surface. These detect the movements of a pointing device (stylus or mouse) and move the cursor on the screen (Figure 4.17). Since it is very accurate, this is used as input to CAD systems and for drawing freehand by artists.

A graphics tablet

Fig 4.17

Touch-sensitive screen

By touching the screen the user can make a selection or move the position of the cursor (Figure 4.18).

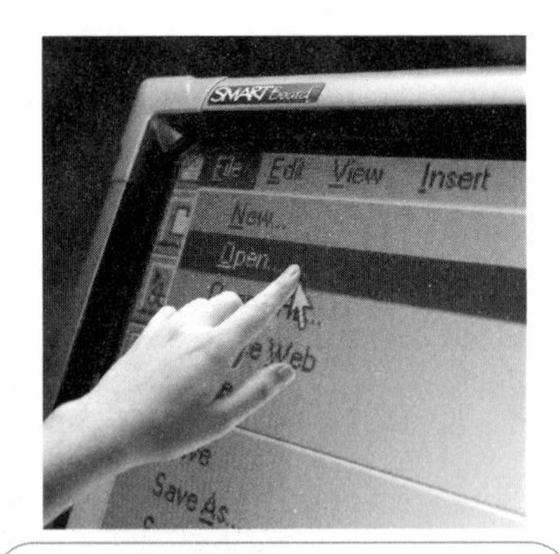

A touch-sensitive screen in use

Fig 4.18

Touch-sensitive screens are simple to operate but are tiring to use for any length of time. They are not suitable for input where precision is needed. They are often used on public information systems.

Keyboard

A keyboard is used to enter text or commands into the computer system. The keyboard has a set of the usual QWERTY keys as well as special command/function keys.

Scanner

A scanner is used to input drawings, illustrations from paper copies or photographs (figure 4.19). A light beam passes over the page and a sensor detects the light being reflected. The image is then stored in the system's memory as binary numbers.

- Using graphics software, an image can be edited before being saved to disk or printed.
- Using character recognition software, text can be scanned in, dropped into a word processing document and then edited.

A flatbed scanner

Fig 4.19

Joystick

This is an input device which is used to play computer games. The joystick moves to give the player control over objects in the game. There are also buttons on the joystick, providing further control options.

Microphone

Microphones are used to input audio data, e.g. a voiceover for a presentation or video.

Digital still camera

When you use a digital still camera to take photographs it captures the light coming in from the lens and converts it into digital form. This it stores in the camera on a flash card or memory stick. Digital cameras have a small screen to display an instant view of the photograph you have just taken. The camera also has editing software which enables you to delete photos that you don't want to keep.

Using the cable and software that comes with the camera you can then transfer the graphic files which hold your photos to your computer where you can process them using graphics software. See page 25 for information on graphics data files used to store photographs.

When choosing between the various digital cameras on the market, what should you look for?

- *Memory capacity.* Digital cameras use memory cards to store your photos before you transfer them to your computer. The storage capacity of the card will affect the number of photographs you can store on the camera.
- *Accuracy.* This can be measured by the number of light-sensitive cells in the camera. You can check this out in an up-to-date magazine. Look for the number of megapixels the camera has.

Digital video camera (camcorder)

Digital video captures moving images in the same way as a digital still camera does. It uses sensors to read light coming in from the lens and then converts it into digital form before storing it in the camera.

Large storage capacity

The key feature of a digital video camera is its large storage capacity. Some use DVD RAM with capacities measured in gigabytes and which can store up to two hours' of video or 2000 or so still photographs.

On-board viewer

To view your video you can use an eyepiece or a small colour liquid-crystal display (LCD) screen. On some models these LCD screens are adjustable and touch-sensitive to allow you to control on-board editing features (e.g. zoom).

Range of features

A digital video camera has a wide range of features to help the user to record: zoom, focus, adjust lighting, switching to taking still pictures, infrared recording for night shots, editing controls and a range of special effects.

Connection to the Internet

Some digital camcorders have an interface that allows them to connect to the Internet using either a mobile phone or an ordinary phone line.

Webcam

A webcam is a digital camera connected to your computer which captures images and displays them in a Web page. The camera is normally connected to a computer using a cable. Software captures pictures from the camera and then loads them on to the website. Webcams can be used to set up video-conferencing (see page 15).

Now you try

1 What type of scanner do you have in school? What have you used it for?
2 Which department in your school is most likely to have a graphics tablet attached to a computer system?
3 Describe a situation where you have used a touch-sensitive screen or seen one being used.
4 Outline *two* advantages of using a digital camera to take photos for a website you are constructing.
5 Using a search engine (see page 12), do a simple Web search for 'webcam'. You will find links to many pages. Write out a short report describing your visit to *two* webcam sites.

Knowledge check 8

1 Which input device are you most likely to use to select an icon?

2 Complete the following, using the words and phrases:
keyboard, gloves with sensors attached, trackball, scanner, microphone, digital camera, graphics tablet, sound card, touch-sensitive screen.
(a) A ________ ______ is used by artists to draw things by hand in the computer.
(b) A ________ is found on some laptops.
(c) A ________ is used to enter text and numbers.
(d) A _______ is used to input a photograph or a drawing into a computer.

(e) A _____ ____ is used to sample sounds and store them in digital form.
(f) You use __________ __________ __________ __________ to pick up things in a virtual world.
(g) With a _____-_______ ______ your computer doesn't even need a keyboard.
(h) You can take a still photograph with a _______ ______ and transfer it to a computer.
(i) You use a _________ to record a voice-over for a multimedia presentation.

Output devices

Printers

Laser printers

A laser printer uses a laser beam to put the image of a page on to a photosensitive drum. It then attracts toner or ink by means of an electrostatic charge before transferring it to paper (Figure 4.20).

The key features of laser printers are:

- they are fast
- they are relatively expensive to buy and run
- printouts are of high quality.

A laser printer and an inkjet printer
Fig 4.20

Inkjet printers

This type of printer sprays ink on to paper to form letters and pictures. The key features of inkjet printers are:

- they are quite cheap
- they are slower than laser printers
- they can produce high-quality printouts
- the cost of ink cartridges is high.

Plotters

Most plotters now use inkjet technology to produce large-scale diagrams, charts and plans (see page 79). Using a computer and plotter is much more efficient than producing accurate, complex drawings by hand.

Comparing printers

- **Speed**. Printers vary in the time they take to print a single page. In its specification a printer's speed will usually be stated as pages per minute (e.g. 6 pages per minute, or ppm for short).
- **Resolution**. The quality of the printout varies according to the number of dots per inch used. You will see printers advertised as using up to, for example, 600 dots per inch (or dpi for short).
- **Costs**
  - Initial cost; the cost of buying the printer.
  - Running costs: cost of toner or ink.

Now you try

Look at some computer magazines or a few websites and then complete the following comparison table.

Printer make/model	*Printer type*	*Speed (ppm)*	*Resolution (dpi)*	*Initial cost*	*Running cost*

Screens

Monitors

A monitor is a screen used to display computer output. Different monitors have different *resolutions*. The higher the resolution the clearer the image. High-resolution monitors are needed for CAD work and art work.

Liquid-crystal display (LCD)

This type of display screen is flat and light (Figure 4.21). It needs little power to operate and so can be run from a battery. LCDs are often found on palmtop and laptop computers because of these features.

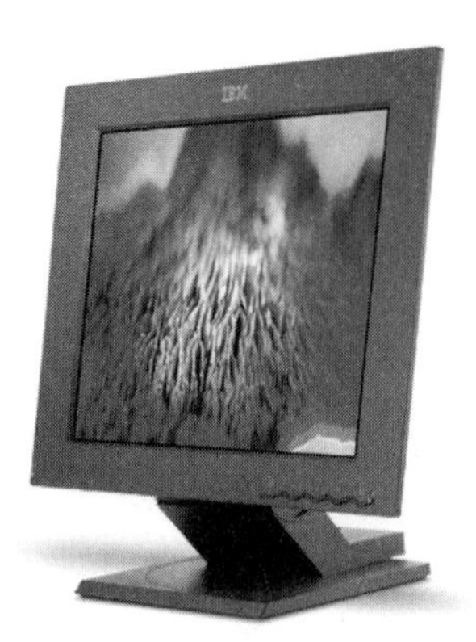

A flat-screen LCD monitor and a laptop with LCD screen

Fig 4.21

A disadvantage is that some LCD screens are not well lit and so can cause eye strain. The newest ones for desktops give much clearer displays.

TFT screens

TFT stands for thin-film transistor and is a type of LCD screen (see page 118) with a tiny transistor to light up each pixel on the screen. Because there are so many transistors the screen can change its displays very quickly, giving a high-quality result. It can handle complex graphics and displays animations clearly, which non-TFT LCD screens do not.

Now you try

1. Write down as many of the details as you can of the printers and monitors that you have on your system.
2. Which department in your school is most likely to have a plotter?
3. If you have access to an LCD screen try running some software with an animation. Does the image have a shadow? Does it handle the moving graphic well? Is it a TFT Screen?

Loudspeakers

Loudspeakers can turn a computer into a multimedia workstation, for use with voice output, multimedia presentations and as an important form of output for video-conferencing.

Speakers vary in quality, from the small variety designed to sit on your desk beside the monitor, to high-quality units with around six individual loudspeakers, giving all-round sound effects (Figure 4.22). One feature to consider is the number of watts of output per channel.

Loudspeakers come in many shapes, sizes and power-handling capabilities

Fig 4.22

Next steps

Sound cards

A sound card changes the sound files held in your computer in digital form into analogue signals which are then sent to the speakers. This is known as digital-to-analogue conversion (see pages 82–83 for more information).

Capturing sound files

When a sound card captures a sound, it takes thousands of samples of the sound waves each second, turning the samples into binary numbers and then storing the data in the computer.

A common sampling frequency is 44 kHz (kilohertz). This means that 44,000 samples are taken and stored each second. A common sampling resolution is 16-bit, which means that each sample is stored as a 16-bit binary number. The consequence is that you can end up with some very big sound files.

Take a simple example of a one-minute sound track sampled at 44 kHz with 16-bits or 2 bytes per sample. This will produce 44,000 × 60 × 2 bytes of storage, which is 5,280,000 bytes. That is a very large file indeed: approximately 5 megabytes in total.

Relieving heavy demands made on the central processor

In the example above, when a file is being output to the loudspeakers the central processor will have to convert 2,640,000 16-bit binary numbers each second into analogue signals. In order to relieve the CPU of the task of processing all this data, most audio cards have a *dedicated* processor, called a 'digital signals processor' or DSP.

Graphics cards

More and more software is hungry for graphics, especially multimedia applications and games with animated 3D graphics. These graphics make lots of demands on system memory and on the central processor's time.

This is where graphics cards come in. They have on-board RAM which is dedicated to storing graphics data: 64 megabytes of RAM on a graphics card is fairly standard.

To relieve the heavy demands which graphics make on the CPU, the latest graphics cards have graphic *accelerators* or *co-processors* which take over the processing of graphics. As it processes the graphics the card takes the digital information about the graphics stored in the RAM and changes it to analogue signals.

The card continuously sends out signals to control the colours and refresh the image on the computer screen. The most modern cards can draw millions of objects per second on a screen, and UXGA cards support 16.8 million colours. Without the accelerators or co-processors this would overburden the processor and slow down the system.

Computer types

Desktop computers

This is probably the type of computer you are using during your course. It is made up of a monitor, keyboard and mouse, and the casing which holds the processor, the memory and the disk drives. It fits neatly on to a desk. In many schools the desktops are connected to a LAN.

Laptop computers

A laptop computer is compact and light, so you can carry it about. This makes it useful for working when travelling. It uses a battery or mains power.

A laptop has a flat LCD screen and a normal keyboard. A mouse or trackball is used to input data (see Figure 4.16).

Palmtop computers

A palmtop computer is about the size of your hand and has a small keyboard. It is powered by a small battery (Figure 4.23). Some types have handwriting recognition and an input pen or stylus.

A palmtop is used for storing data (e.g. word processing and database files), keeping diary appointments and carrying out financial calculations. Some are even merging with mobile phone technology to let you access the Internet. A palmtop stores data on a flashcard.

A palmtop computer
Fig 4.23

Mainframe

A mainframe computer is a large and very powerful computer with lots of processing power, plenty of main memory and backing storage.

Mainframes often have many users who are connected to the system using terminals. Businesses like banks and other large organisations use them to process and store their data (see page 138).

Knowledge check 9

1 Complete the following, using the words and phrases:
plotter, LCD screen, monitor, laser printer, inkjet printer, voice output.

(a) A _____ _______ uses optical technology to produce high-quality printouts.
(b) A _______ is used to display the output on your desktop computer.
(c) ______ printers are cheap to buy and produce reasonably good quality printouts but are comparatively slow.
(d) A laptop uses an ___ ______ because it is lightweight and can be powered from a battery.
(e) _____ ______ is suitable for people who have difficulty reading screens.
(f) You could find a _______ attached to the computer in an architect's office.

2 Write down *three* important facts about (a) a palmtop, (b) a laptop, and (c) a desktop computer.

3 What would a palmtop be used for?

4 What advantage is there in using a laptop?

5 What advantages does a desktop computer have?

Credit questions

6 Do a search on the Web for sound cards. Pick one and write up a short report on its main features. Pick the sound card on your own computer for the report, if you know what it is.

7 Why is it important for a graphics card to have its own processor dedicated to processing graphics data?

Next steps

Multimedia

Multimedia systems incorporate and integrate sound, animated images, video and graphics within a single user-friendly computer interface. They are used:

- to provide learning systems so that learners can interact with and access text, video images, sound tracks and graphics
- for interactive information systems
- for displaying multimedia Web pages
- for games.

A typical modern multimedia specification is:

- a fast central processor: 2 gigahertz and above
- at least 500 megabytes of RAM
- a 40 gigabyte hard disk
- a high-speed CD-ROM drive
- sound and graphics interfaces
- a set of speakers
- a good-quality colour monitor.

With a good mltimedia system you should also use:

- input devices such as a scanner, digital camera and digtal video camera
- output devices such as surround sound speakers and perhaps a data projector.

Now you try

The typical specification of a multimedia system given above might be out of date by the time you reach this task. Write out the specification for the latest multimedia desktop computer system you can find in magazines or on the Internet.

Virtual reality

A virtual-reality system creates the illusion that the user is inside the world created by the virtual-reality software. The user feels part of that world and can move around in it and manipulate it. Virtual-reality systems are used for training as well as for entertainment (Figure 4.23). But how do they work?

Input

Virtual-reality systems use a range of *input devices* which are built into special gloves, helmets and even suits which the user wears. Examples are ultrasound transmitters in gloves and suits which pinpoint the user's movements, and strips built into gloves that vary their resistance when bent. These sensors send data to the processor which uses it to detect the user's movements.

Output

The illusion of being inside the computer's world is created by *output devices* built into the headset, usually a helmet or goggles. There will be a pair of miniature high-quality screens that produce a realistic three-dimensional environment, and a pair of high-quality speakers that produce all-round sound. The output is so effective that the user is convinced he or she is inside the computer's world.

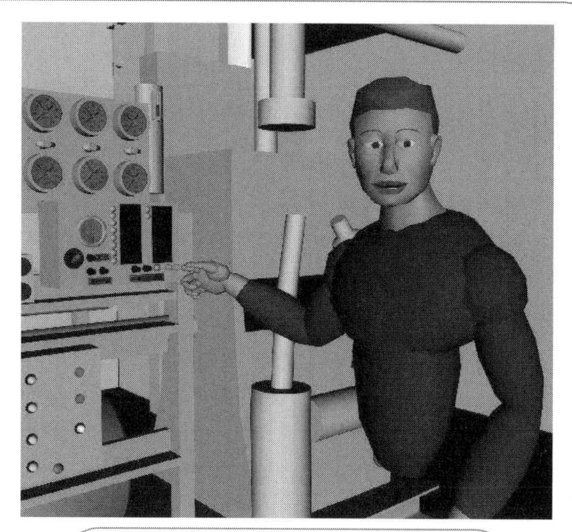

A still graphic from a virtual-reality system used for training

Fig 4.24

Specialised input devices for disabled people

Biosensors

Biosensors are used in special input devices for people with a disability. Biosensors detect slight changes in parts of the body and use this as input to a computer.

- Muscle sensors detect electrical activity in muscles.
- Eye sensors detect eye movements

Special keyboards have been designed for disabled users, and there are also special screens available for people with speech difficulties (Figure 4.25).

Disabled users can also use a head tracking mouse. A device attached to the computer transmits signals to a reflector on the user's head, allowing the user to control the cursor by moving their head.

People with disabilities are catered for with special keyboards and screens

Fig 4.25

Specialised output devices for disabled people

Speech output
People with reading difficulties can use software to speak the text of their files out to them. There are handheld text to speech readers which can hold thousands of pages of text and can read continuously for hours.

Ultrasound and infrared output
People with disabilities can use computer systems to control appliances around the home. Computer systems fitted with infrared and ultrasound output devices can be used to control appliances such as a television, radio, lights and CD players.

Knowledge check 10

1. Describe a multimedia system.
2. What is a multimedia system used for?
3. List the parts of a multimedia system.
4. Name the sensors used as input to a virtual-reality system.
5. Where are these sensors located?
6. Describe the output from a multimedia system.
7. Describe the effect of a virtual-reality system.
8. Describe the job of a sound card.
9. Describe *two* input devices that would be suitable for people with a disability.

End of unit progress check

Questions

1. What is an operating system? 2
2. The designer decides that the autopilot computer on an aircraft will have a real-time system. What are the designer's reasons for this choice? 2
3. How could you tell the difference between a program written in machine code and one written in a high-level language? 2
4. When you type in a formula for a spreadsheet does your computer store it in ROM or RAM? 1
5. When you switch off your computer what happens to the data held in RAM? 1
6. How does your computer store the letter 'A'? 1
7. You need a small computer to record appointments. You want one to fit in your pocket. What kind should you buy? 1

8 A village in the Highlands, set in beautiful scenery, wants to attract tourists to the area. How could the installation of a webcam help boost visitor numbers? 2

9 A kitchen designer wants a good-quality printout of her work. What output device should she use? 1

10 Your friend has a lot of trouble finding files on his hard disk because there are dozens of file icons scattered everywhere. What could you do to help him? 2

11 Explain why LCD screens are used on laptops. 3

Foundation/general total 18 marks

Credit questions

12 The electricity company has to constantly produce batches of bills for its customers and still be able to answer customer enquiries using its computer. What type of operating system would be most suitable? Give reasons for your answer. 2

13 Using the example of mouse clicks to select files, explain how an operating system provides an HCI for the user. 2

14 A disabled friend asks for advice about special input devices to help him input data to his computer. Describe two devices he could consider using. 2

15 You use a virtual-reality system and feel that you have been inside the computer's world. What output and input devices are having this effect? 4

16 You ask your teacher to print out the record which holds your grades from the class database held on a hard disk. What type of access will the system use to find your record? 1

17 What is the name of the memory units inside a processor? 1

18 Your friend buys a new game for her desktop computer. It has excellent 3D graphics and animations, but sometimes the graphics seem jerky and lose clarity. She thinks the problem lies in the graphics card. What should she look out for when buying a new graphics card? 2

19 What would the job of the control unit be when you want some data from the computer's memory? 1

20 What is the function of a device driver? 1

21 A program is written to control a robot arm. Which type of translator would be best: a compiler or an interpreter? Give *two* reasons for your answer. 3

22 You have produced a multimedia presentation which is interactive and allows you to move through it as you see fit using link buttons. It has lots of graphics, video clips and sound files, as well as text. You want to save it to backing storage and still be able to update it in the future.

(a) Why would a re-writable CD be a suitable storage medium for the presentation? 1

(b) When the presentation is running, the system needs to access specific files from time to time. Why would sequential access not be suitable for this? 1

23 What would be the storage requirements for a small black and white graphic measuring 3 inches square with 200 pixels per inch? 2

Credit total 23 marks

Unit 5

Commercial data processing

What you will read about in this unit

- What is commercial data processing (CDP)?
- The data processing cycle
- Collecting, preparing and entering data
- Checking the data
- Processing the data
- Storing data files
- Multi-user databases
- Sequential access and direct/random access to data
- Data security
- Output of information
- Hardware
- Jobs within CDP
- E-commerce
- Costs of commercial data processing
- Computer crime and fraud

What is commercial data processing (CDP)?

Commercial data processing is the use of computers to gather, store, process and output data on a large scale. It is used by banks, mail-order firms and all organisations which have to deal with hundreds of thousands or even millions of pieces of data each day.

CDP systems are used for:

- stock control – keeping track of what is in stock
- producing payrolls – making up wage slips
- keeping track of orders
- producing invoices
- monitoring payments and withdrawals
- processing application forms
- producing statements.

Using a CDP system makes it possible for a businesses to keep accurate up-to-date records of, in some cases, hundreds of thousands of customers. They can use this data to communicate instantly and accurately with their customers about orders, sales, invoices and payments. This in turn boosts the efficiency of the business. Without a CDP system a large-scale business such as a bank simply could not compete with its rivals.

Why are commercial data processing systems better than manual systems?

- *They can cope with high volumes of data*. Some businesses produce thousands of wage slips, banks handle millions of withdrawals each day.
- *They handle repetitive work easily*. Imagine how difficult and repetitive it would be if you were asked to produce 1000 payslips by hand.
- *They process data at high speed*, much faster than any human could operate.
- *They are very accurate and eliminate mistakes*, providing all the data is input correctly. People make mistakes.
- *They offer instant access to the data*. It takes a fraction of a second for a CDP system to find data and display it on a screen, outperforming a human with ease.

Next steps

- *Data is available for instant use by many people*, once it has been entered into the system. The CDP system instantly makes the data available to everyone with access to the system (Figure 5.1).

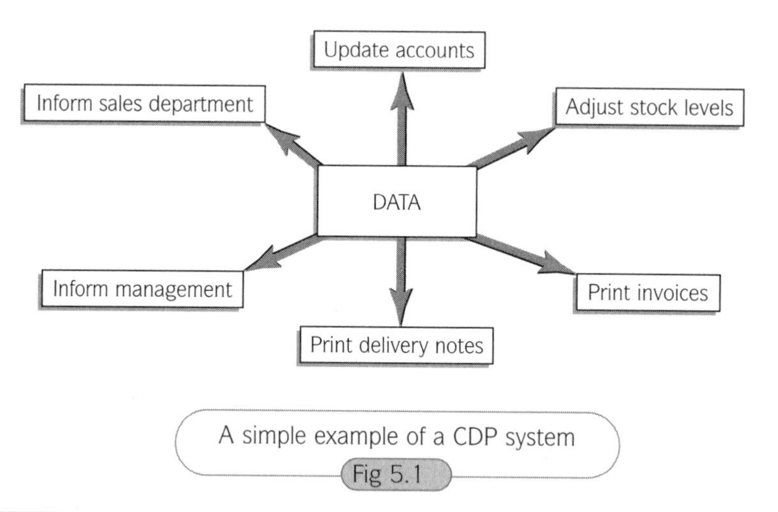

A simple example of a CDP system

Fig 5.1

Now you try

How would a mail-order business use commercial data processing?

Next steps

Management information

Managing a business is made easier by having all the business data available on the CDP system. Management have instant access to up-to-date and accurate data on matters such as sales patterns, stock levels and the finances of the business. This data will form the basis of day-to-day management decisions. Because these decisions are being made on the basis of up-to-date information provided by the system, they are likely to be more accurate than those based on data provided by a manual system. All of this helps ensure business efficiency.

Now you try

What would you say to convince the management of a mail-order business that they should be using a commercial data processing system?

Data and information: the difference

Before you read any further, make sure you understand the difference between the terms 'data' and 'information' as used in CDP. A piece of data is a fact, an item of information which on its own has little meaning – for example the cost of an item sold in a store. When lots of pieces of data have been collected and processed it has much more meaning and is known as 'information'. For example, the costs of all items sold in a month could be made into a graph to show the pattern of sales in that month.

The data processing cycle

Commercial data processing is organised around the data processing cycle. This has three main stages:

- collecting, preparing and entering the data
- processing and storing the data
- information output.

Collecting, preparing and entering data

Magnetic stripes

Data can be stored on a strip of magnetic tape on the back of a card (Figure 5.2). When the card is passed through a card-reader the data is entered directly into the system. They are used on bank cards and credit cards. Magnetic stripes are:

- simple to operate
- a quick and accurate way to enter account details into the system.

A magnetic stripe on the back of a card

Fig 5.2

Magnetic-ink character recognition (MICR)

MICR is used on cheques. Special magnetised ink is used on cheques to print details such as the account number and the sort code. The MICR-reader uses these details to sort and record the cheques. Using MICR has advantages:

- the cheques are processed at high speed (an automatic MICR-reader processes thousands in an hour)
- MICR makes it difficult to forge cheques.

Barcodes

Items can have a printed barcode with all the details needed for a computer system to identify them. A barcode is a combination of black and white bars (Figure 5.3). The barcode-reader reflects laser light from the barcode and produces binary data. All the data on the code is entered into the system in a fraction of a second. The advantages are:

- speed of entry
- accuracy.

The barcode also enables a computer to instantly identify an item. It is such an efficient way of entering data it is used on virtually everything you buy, from books to beans.

A barcode
Fig 5.3

Now you try

1. Where would you expect to find people using magnetic stripes?
2. Why do you think barcodes are so popular?
3. Complete this sentence: 'If banks didn't have MICR on their cheques . . . . . .'.

Mark sense cards

These are documents with a grid printed on them. The user makes a selection from a list by putting a mark into a 'box' on the grid opposite the choice. The data is then read into the system using an optical mark-reader which recognizes the user's pen or pencil mark.

Mark sense cards are used in multiple-choice tests, lottery tickets, and questionnaires. The advantages are:

- they are simple for the users
- they are fast (readers can process 10 thousand mark sense cards in an hour)
- the data entry is very accurate.

Next steps

Smartcards

A smartcard is a card with a *microchip* and *memory circuits* inserted on the card. Some of the memory holds data permanently and some can be updated as needed. This means smartcards can store data and process simple software.

Next steps continued

Security

You could use the storage capacity of a smartcard to hold a digital fingerprint or a voiceprint. This could be used to:

- identify the user
- gain access to secure parts of buildings
- access data held on a network
- provide a secure way of accessing money (by being used as a debit or credit card)

A smartcard can also be programmed to check that the card-reading device is authorised and not a fake. This could help to eliminate card theft.

Updating smartcards

The data on a smartcard can be updated every time it is used. This means that it can be used as a means of electronically storing cash credits: a type of electronic wallet. Smartcards can be used to control access to and charges for parking places and even use of motorways.

Optical character recognition

Optical character recognition (OCR) reads text directly into a computer system. It reads the characters by reflecting light from the page and then comparing the shapes it reads with the sets of characters stored in memory. It works best with special *optical fonts* (Figure 5.4).

OCR is used mainly by businesses that need to input text from documents into a computer system – such as from turnaround documents (see above). You can use OCR on your scanner at home or in school, if you have the correct software.

The main advantage of OCR is that there is no need to retype data into the computer, so saving considerable time.

ABCDEFGHIJKLMN
OPQRSTUVWXYZ
0123456789

Special optical fonts designed for use with OCR

Fig 5.4

Now you try

1 Write down the reasons for (a) a market research company using mark sense cards, and (b) a bank using MICR.

Credit question

2 Write down the reasons for using a smartcard to ensure secure access to a bank account.

Knowledge check 1

1. Give *three* examples of where commercial data processing is used.
2. Give *four* reasons, with examples, why CDP systems are used.
3. What is the difference between data and information?
4. Copy out the table and complete it by entering the appropriate word or phrase from the following:
   barcodes; magnetic stripes; MICR; collecting, preparing and entering the data; mark sense card

The first stage of the data processing cycle	
Magnetised ink, used on cheques and read into the computer by a special reader	
Magnetic stripe on the back of a card, holding account details	
Pen or pencil marks on a card can be read as data into a computer	
Black and white lines which represent numbers	

Credit questions

5. Complete the sentence:
   _ _ _ involves reading text in using a scanner and character recognition software.
6. Complete the sentence:
   A _____ ____ is a card that has its own microchip and memory.

Checking the data

Presence check

This checks to make sure that a data item has not been completely left out.

Range check

Range checks make sure the data entered is within a certain range. Examples of range checks are:

- a month entered as part of a date is from 1 to 12
- a percentage exam result is between 0 and 100.

Field length check

This checks that the correct amount of numbers or characters has been entered. There are usually four numbers in a PIN for cash machines, so if you enter three numbers it will reject your entry and ask you to try again.

Field or data type check

This checks to make sure data is of the correct *type*. A field type check will detect numbers where text should be, and vice versa. If numbers are entered into a name field it will be spotted as an error (Figure 5.5).

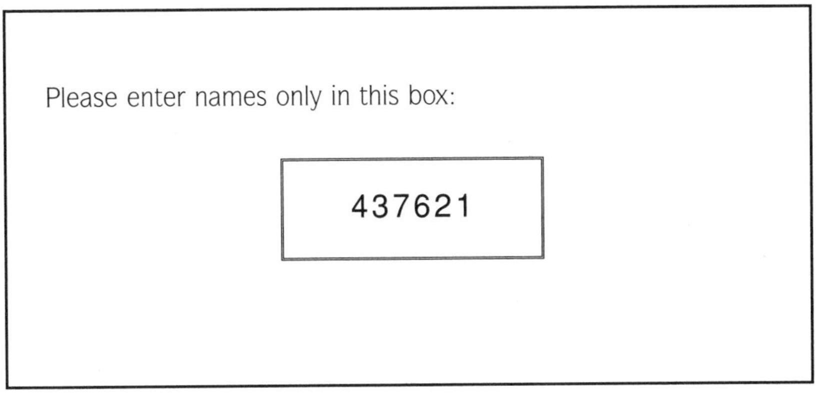

Please enter names only in this box:

437621

In this case the user has entered numbers instead of letters in a name box

Fig 5.5

Check digits

A check digit is a number usually located at the end of a series of a numbers, for example the last number of a barcode.

When you enter a sequence of numbers into the computer it calculates the check digit in order to make sure that the other numbers in a sequence have been entered properly.

Now you try

Imagine you are setting up a Web page to register people as on-line customers for a mail-order company. What types of check would you include (a) to make sure their names are typed in the correct box and not in their account number box, (b) to make sure they entered their account number properly, and (c) to make sure that people didn't order too large a number of any one item?

Next steps

Verification

When data is entered at a keyboard by an operator, it is checked to make sure that it has been entered correctly. There are two types of verification check:

- Once the data has been entered it is displayed on the screen and the operator is asked to confirm that the details are correct by a simple 'Is this correct Y/N?' message. If the data is on a form, the operator will read it again to make sure it is correct. If the data is being telephoned in, the operator will ask the caller whether the details are correct. Only then will the data be entered.
- In a double-entry system, two different operators type in the data. The computer accepts the information for processing only when both entries are identical.

Validation

Validation checks are then made by the system itself, which uses software made to ensure that data is of the required type and in the correct place.

Knowledge check 2

1 Copy out the table and then complete it by selecting from the following phrases: *range check, field type check, presence check, check digit, field length check.*

Checking that numbers and characters have been entered in the correct places	
Checking that the entry is not too big for the field	
Checking that the entry is in a specified range (e.g. 1 to 100)	
The computer calculates this number in order to make sure that the other numbers in a sequence have been entered properly	
Checks to make sure that an entry has been made into a field	

Credit questions

2 What is data verification? Give *two* examples.

3 What is the key difference between data verification and data validation?

Storing data files

The data is stored in electronic files. Each file is made up of records and fields (see page 49).

Data files are constantly being **updated**. This means that the data in the file is altered in order to bring the contents of the file up to date and make sure it is accurate.

Now you try

1 What type of data would be stored in files by (a) a mail-order firm, (b) a payroll system, and (c) a bank?

2 When would the data held on file by a bank be updated?

Processing the data

You have to know about *interactive processing*. With interactive processing, each transaction updates the master file immediately, as soon as the data is entered. For example, immediate updates are necessary for airline reservation systems, and for cashline systems in a bank.

Now you try

Copy out and complete the chart below to show examples of the use of interactive processing systems.

Interactive processing system
Booking a holiday with a travel agent

Next steps

Multi-user databases

A multi-user database is one that allows many people to access the data at one time using a LAN, a WAN or even the Web. Many multi-user databases are specific to an organisation – such as a bank – but some can be accessed freely through the Web.

Many multi-user databases use a database management system, known as a DBMS.

We can divide multi-user databases into:

- relatively simple databases with comparatively few users which might run on a LAN
- large databases used by big businesses
- databases accessible across the Web.

Web-based multi-user databases

There are multi-user databases which you can access over the Web. Examples are databases on musicians, recordings and compositions. Once you have logged on to the site you use your browser to request some data. Your request goes to a web-server where the database server software resides. The web-server then changes the report from the database into a form your browser can read before sending it back to your system across the Internet.

Advantages of multi-user databases

Multi-user databases enable businesses and organisations to:

- have many people working on the complex task of updating the information held on a database
- give employees instant easy access to the data they need for their work
- support instant on-line access to account information for customers.

Web-based multi-user databases are an important source of information for anyone with Internet access, for leisure, education or business purposes.

Security on a multi-user database

In a Web-based database that is not open to the public, there is obviously a need to organise access to the data. Using a system of IDs and passwords it is possible for the database manager or network manager to control the level of access. Each individual in an organisation will be assigned rights which will allow the person to see and perhaps update specific parts of the database.

Next steps continued

Sequential access and direct/random access to data

Sequential access

When a system uses sequential access to data it goes to each record in a file one after another in sequence. There is more information on this in the Computer systems unit (see page 99). Sequential access is best suited to batch processing where all or most of the records in a file are updated in a batch (e.g. when processing a payroll). Magnetic tape is a sequential-access medium.

Direct/random access

A system using direct/random access goes directly to the data it requires (see page 99). It is best suited to interactive processing which requires immediate access to data.
Any CDP system which needs to update the master files immediately will use direct/random access. Examples of CDP systems using this form of access are banks updating customer withdrawals and payments, and ticket booking systems.

Now you try

1 Copy out the table below and add further examples of the use of sequential and direct/random access.

Sequential access	*Direct/random access*
Payroll system for producing wage slips	Ticket booking system

2 Outline how a large-scale multi-user database operates.

3 What advantages are there for a business in having a multi-user database?

Data security

All master files must be protected against data corruption or loss, and unauthorised access (hacking).

IDs and passwords

All users are given identity codes (IDs) and passwords. These make it difficult to access files without proper authority. Advanced ID measures include the use of smartcards to store fingerprint or voiceprint information (see page 130).

Data encryption

Encryption means putting data into a codified form. If anyone without authority accesses the data it will be meaningless without the key to the code.

Auditing software

Auditing software traces everything that happens to a file: updating, saving, printing. It records when data was accessed or changed and can help to trace hackers.

Other security measures

- Fit each computer terminal with a lock and key.
- Limit access to rooms with computer terminals, using security locks.
- Use terminals without floppy or CD drives, to make it more difficult for viruses to be transferred.

Knowledge check 3

1 Complete these sentences:

(a) Files are made up of _______.

(b) Records are made up of _______.

(c) Fields hold items of ____ .

(d) Interactive processing _______ the data files ___________ . It is used by banks to update _____ after people withdraw money from cashpoints.

Files, immediately, updates

2 Why are regular backups made?

3 List *three* system security measures and *three* other security measures that can be taken to protect data.

Credit questions

4 Why is sequential access suitable for a computer used by an electricity supply company when producing customers' bills?

5 Why is random/direct access suitable for the computer controlling a bank's cashline machine?

6 A mail-order company processes thousands of items of data each hour of the working day. The sales staff, accounts staff and management all need to be able to access and update customer records simultaneously. Explain in detail the structure of the database system needed.

Output of information

Monitors

Monitors of various types are used to view the information derived from data. Monitors are discussed on page 118.

Printers

CDP systems can use a range of printers. When the CDP system has to print out thousands of documents (e.g. account statements), high-speed laser types are used. These have print speeds of around 40 pages per minute and can produce 100,000 pages per month. When a small amount of printing is needed, a standard office laser printer would be adequate (Figure 5.6).

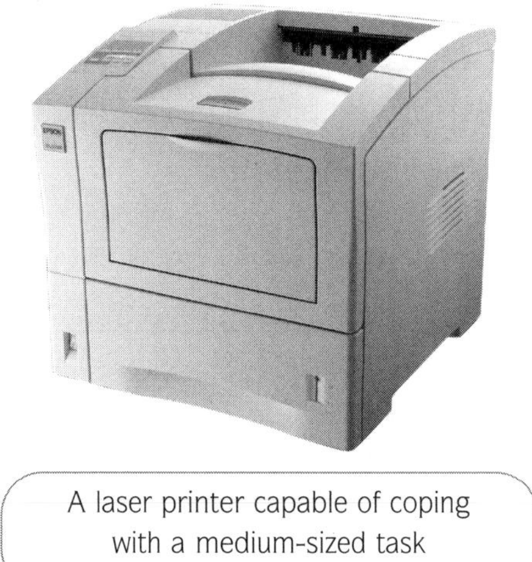

A laser printer capable of coping with a medium-sized task

Fig 5.6

Next steps

Output to file

The output does not have to be to a paper copy. Output can also be to an electronic file. This means that the data file is saved to backing storage where it is available for future use.

Hardware

Commercial data processing generally uses *mainframe computers* that have:

- very fast processors
- large internal memory capacity
- large backing storage capability
- many terminals.

Figure 5.7 shows a small mainframe.

A small mainframe computer used in CDP

Fig 5.7

Now you try

Use the Internet to find details and illustrations of:

- monitors
- printers
- mainframes.

Jobs within CDP

CDP systems create a range of jobs for people to do.

Systems analysts

Systems analysts work out the tasks that the CDP system has to carry out. They decide on the hardware that is needed, and design the necessary software. When the software has been written, the systems analysts make sure the system is set up and tested correctly.

Programmers

Programmers take the software design and write the actual software that runs the CDP system.

Engineers

Computer engineers set up the hardware and do any maintenance that is needed, such as replacing malfunctioning or obsolete parts.

Network managers

A network manager sets up user IDs, controls access to files, sets up links to printers, installs software, controls access to websites on the Internet, and establishes and maintains network security.

E-commerce

E-commerce is the use of computer networks to allow people to buy and sell things.

The Internet is increasingly used for e-commerce. Using the Internet you can go on-line shopping. You can view products, put them in your on-line basket, pay for them and have them delivered to your house. You can even trade in stocks and shares.

You can buy something at an on-line auction. You can bid for items on sale. If your bid wins, you can pay on-line and have the goods delivered.

The benefits of e-commerce are:

- the customer can shop from home without having to travel
- goods are delivered to your door.

For a business, another benefit is that it can have customers worldwide. It can take orders and payments worldwide.

There is a disadvantage of e-commerce. Criminals continually look for ways to steal peoples' credit card data as they pay for things on-line.

On-line shopping

On-line shopping means using the Internet to buy things. How does it work? You visit a website, look at the goods, read about them and, if you like them, you place them in your virtual shopping basket. You then complete an order form with your details. When you have finished you have to pay for them using a credit card or debit card.

On-line banking

On-line banking lets you process your financial affairs over the Internet. How does it work? Using your computer and modem, or mobile phone or Internet TV, you log on to a bank's website. Then you can:

- view your balance and check your transactions 24 hours a day
- make money transfers and pay bills

- send secure messages to the bank
- arrange an overdraft
- set up e-savings
- access a wide range of services and products: check out mortgage deals, set up loans or insurance.

The banks guarantee the security of the operations, so if anyone hacks into your account and steals money it will be refunded.

Electronic funds transfer at the point of sale

Electronic funds transfer (EFT)

This uses computers to transfer money electronically from one bank account to another. When you pay for your groceries in the supermarket using EFT, the cost of your groceries is taken from your account and put into the supermarket's account.

The EFT terminal sends a request through to the customer's bank to transfer the money from the customer's account to the account of the supermarket. If there is enough money in the account the transfer is made by the computer system.

Advantages for the customer

In this way a customer can pay for goods without having to go to a bank and draw out cash.

Advantages for the business

The business gets the money paid directly into its account without having to handle cash, count it and take it to a bank.

Point-of-sale (POS) terminals

A POS terminal in a shop or supermarket is linked to a computer system. The POS terminal can be used to pay for goods using EFT. The computer:

- uses barcodes to read in the customer's goods.
- calculates and prints the bill/receipt.
- sends the data to a computer which adjusts the stock levels and totals the amount being paid in at the terminals.

Advantages for the customer

- The use of barcodes speeds up the selling process.
- The shelves will be well stocked thanks to the stock control system of which POS is a key part.
- Receipts have all the details and there are fewer mistakes.

Advantages for the business

The pricing of goods is done by the computer system, saving staff time. The system also keeps a record of all sales, helping to manage stock and finances. The shelves should always be well-stocked.

Costs of commercial data processing

Any computer system involves costs, and CDP systems are no exception.

Initial costs

These are the costs involved at the beginning, when the system is being set up. Examples are:

- paying for the hardware
- paying for the software
- the systems analyst's fee.

Running costs

These are the costs of keeping the system going:

- maintaining the hardware and software
- staff wages
- printing costs
- bills for power and telephones.

Now you try

1. In what ways does EFT benefit a mail-order company and its customers?
2. The initial costs and running costs involved in a commercial data processing system are high. Why do businesses think it's worth the costs?

Knowledge check 4

1 Complete this sentence:
Monitors are used to _______ the ____ on a computer system.

2 Why are high-speed laser printers used in CPD?

3 List *four* important facts about a mainframe computer.

4 Copy out and then complete the table using these words:
software, check, maintenance, set up, design the software, control access, printers, websites

Systems analysts	Work out the tasks that the CDP system has to carry out Decide on the hardware that is needed ______ ___ ________ Make sure the system is set up and tested correctly
Programmers	Write the ________ which runs the CDP system
Engineers	___ __ the hardware and do any ___________ that is needed – e.g. repairing disk drives
Network managers	Set up user IDs, _______ _______ to files, set up links to ________, install software, control access to ________ on the Internet

5 How does EFT operate?

6 How does EFT benefit a customer?

7 Where would you find a POS terminal?

8 Why do businesses use POS?

9 List *four* things you can do using on-line banking.

10 What is e-commerce?

11 What advantages are there for anyone shopping on the Internet?

12 What is the difference between initial and running costs? Give *two* examples of each.

Next steps

Computer crime and fraud

If criminals can breach the security surrounding the data held on CDP systems they can commit a wide range of crimes, such as these:

- copy sensitive personal data
- steal the access codes and IDs which allow access to people's accounts
- steal money from accounts
- change data held on the system
- disable the system using viruses
- make counterfeit magnetic stripe cards to access bank accounts.

The effect of these crimes can cause havoc with people's accounts and disrupt the smooth running of businesses.

Security, privacy and the law

Commercial data processing systems have to ensure that they keep within the Data Protection Act and other legislation relating to the use of computer systems. This legislation and other related security and privacy issues are dealt with in the General purpose packages unit (page 70).

End of unit progress check

Questions

1 Complete the following:
Reasons for using a CDP system
(a) It can handle large _______ of information.
(b) It gives instant ______ to information.
(c) It can handle ___________ tasks. **3**

2 Describe how a bank might use magnetic stripes and MICR as ways of inputting data into its computer system. **2**

3 Label this graphic:

1

4 Kayley's Mail Order updates its stock files immediately the orders come in by phone.
(a) What type of processing system is its computer using? 1
(b) Why does it use this type of processing? 1

5 Why does the Bank of Scotland use MICR? 1

6 What type of computer would the Scotia Bank use to process its data: a laptop, a desktop or a mainframe? Give *two* reasons for your answer. 3

7 State *one* possible problem that can arise when people use the Internet for shopping? 1

8 Name *one* advantage Internet banking gives (a) customers and (b) the bank. 2

9 Why do people find EFT so convenient? 1

10 Complete the following:
(a) As a __________ you would work alongside the systems analyst and write and test the software she designs. 1
(b) As an ________ will install and maintain all the computer hardware. 1

11 Once a business has paid for its computer system and the software, it doesn't have to worry about any other costs in the future. Is this true? Give reasons for your answer. 2

Foundation/general total 20 marks

Credit questions

12 The Kayley's Mail Order computer uses an interactive processing system. Why does it also need to have random/direct access to all its data? 2

13 Each month the Scotia Bank prints out statements for all its customers. Describe the method its computer system should use to access the customer records. 2

14 Explain the difference between verification and validation, in one simple sentence. 2

15 Hackers are breaching Scotia Bank's security regularly and taking money from accounts. How could the replacing of customers' magnetic stripe cards with smartcards help tighten up security? 2

16 Kayley's Mail Order is having trouble with its ordering system. The following errors are being made when data is being entered:
(a) some data items are left out completely
(b) text is often entered where there should be only numbers
(c) numbers are entered that are far too big for the orders
(d) account numbers are being entered incorrectly.
Suggest a solution for each type of error. 4

17 Suggest a way in which Kayley's Mail Order can enter the data on application forms other than by having it typed in at the keyboard. 1

18 Write a paragraph explaining why having a multi-access database is so important to people managing a large business like Kayley's Mail Order. 3

Credit total 16 marks

Problem solving

In this section we will

- Explain different types of problem solving questions.
- Go through examples in detail.
- Suggest strategies you can use.
- Ask you to finish off problem solving solutions that have been almost completed.
- Ask you to answer problems of each type and help you check your answers.

Types of problem solving questions

You need to be able to answer a wide range of problem solving questions.

Outlining solutions

One type of problem solving question asks you to outline solutions to a problem. Lets look at an example.

Example

What would be the most suitable way to ***backup*** *a* ***1 Mbyte file*** *so that it can* ***easily be carried in your schoolbag****?*

How would you answer this? Firstly, read the question carefully, you need to pick out the most important or key ideas. In this example they have been put into bold for you.

Key Ideas	*How they point to the solution*
Make a backup	You have to make a copy of the file
The file is 1 Mbyte in size	It is small enough to fit on a floppy disk
It has to be easily carried in your bag	Both a floppy disc and a writable CD are easily carried about

The answer

The answer we are looking for is to backup the file onto a floppy disk because the file is small enough to fit onto a floppy disk, and because a floppy disk is small and easily slips into your bag. Why not use a writable CD? Because the CD holds 650 Mbytes and so most of its storage space would be left empty.

Problem solving tips

- Read the question carefully.
- Pick out the key ideas.
- Ask yourself how the key ideas point to the solution.

Now you try

1 You have put together a website on your favourite movie star. The site is made up of multimedia Web pages with many linked sound and graphic files. *It is quite large: about 500 Mbytes. You will need to update it each week* as new movies are released and as news breaks. What is the best type of backup?

Key Idea	*How it points to the solution*
It is 500 Mbytes in size	
It needs to be updated regularly	

2 The hard disk on your desktop holds 30 Gbytes. What would be the most efficient way to back it up? Give reasons for your answer.

Explaining the reasons behind your solution

Some questions ask you to explain the reasons for your solution to a problem. Here's an example.

Example

A computer is used for booking airline tickets. Which would be most suitable: ***Batch*** *or* ***Interactive*** *processing? Give reasons for your answer.*

How do you begin to answer this? Firstly, you need to know about *Batch* and *Interactive* processing.

Batch processing	Gathers information it needs over a period of time and stores it in a transaction file It then processes all the jobs one after another at a given time e.g. at the end of the day, the end of the week, or the end of the month
Interactive processing	It processes the data immediately without the delay involved in batch processing

Then you need to think about the information held in the question which points towards the answer. Booking a ticket must be done immediately. If there was a delay and the jobs were done later there could be double bookings.

The answer

The computer used for booking the ticket must use interactive processing because it must be done immediately. If a batch system were used there would be a delay between entering the data and the booking being processed. This would lead to errors in the booking system, e.g. double bookings.

Problem solving tips

- You need to know about the topics on the course and think about the information held in the question before you start to form your answer.
- Don't forget to use *because*, and state your reasons clearly.

Now you try

A mail order business needs to be able to tell customers about stock levels while they are on the phone. It also needs to do large runs of invoices and account statements throughout the day. What kind of operating system is needed? *Give your reasons.*

Batch processing	Gathers information it needs over a period of time and stores it in a transaction file It then processes all the jobs one after another at a given time e.g. at the end of the day, the end of the week, or the end of the month
Interactive processing	It processes the data immediately without the delay involved in batch processing
Interactive processing with background job capability	This system processes data interactively while carrying on batch processing when the processor is not dealing with interactive requests

Setting out the stages in your solution

Some problem solving questions ask you to set out the stages or steps involved in your solution. Here's an example.

Example

You are asked to design an automated system to control the humidity and temperature in a large greenhouse. What would the system consist of? Be as detailed as you can.

How do you answer this? Just like in the earlier examples you need to:

- read the question carefully
- pick out the key ideas
- think how the key ideas point to the steps in a complex solution.

Before you begin, you need to think about all the parts that go to make up an automated system. Refer to pages 80–82 if you need to.

Key Ideas	*How this points to the solution*
Its an automated system	It will need a computer and software
It needs to control *humidity*	It will need humidity sensors
It needs to control *temperature*	It will need sensors for the temperature The sensors will have to send their data to the computer
It needs to control *equipment/mechanisms to regulate the temperature and humidity*	It will need an A/D and a D/A converter It will need to send signals to the motors which control the heating, ventilation and water sprinkler

The answer

- The system would consist of a controlling computer system on which was installed software written in a control language.
- The system would have humidity and temperature sensors.
- These sensors would feedback their data to the controlling computer.
- The system would have A/D converters between the sensors and the processor, and D/A converters between the processor and the motors controlling ventilation, heating and water sprinklers.

Problem solving tips

- Before you begin solving a problem you need to have a very good knowledge of all the topics on the course.
- Set out the different parts to your answer clearly and in the correct order.

Now you try

1 An insurance company wants to produce a brochure to give to potential customers. It will contain text, graphics, statistics, and graphs. How would this brochure be put together using an integrated package?

2 You work for a company that checks out people's credit ratings. Your boss asks you to take responsibility for making sure that the business does not break any laws regarding the storing of personal data on computer. What steps would you take to make sure you stay within the principles of the Data Protection Act?

3 A lawyer needs to keep records of her clients' cases, sometimes for years. Printed copies of the records take up too much space. Explain in detail how the lawyer could solve her long-term storage problem.

Improving solutions

Sometimes you will be given a solution and asked to think of ways to improve it. Here's an example.

Example

A book club has a computerised ordering system. Orders are entered at a keyboard from forms or phone orders. A systems analyst is asked to suggest ways of automating the entry of the book orders to speed things up and cut down on errors. What improvements could the systems analyst come up with?

How do you begin to answer this type of question? Think about the solution that you have been asked to improve. You need to know about different ways of inputting the data such as:

Keyboard data entry	This relies on the operator's skills at the keyboard It also relies on the operator to verify the data before storing it in the system Both these factors make it possible for mistakes to occur
Turnaround documents	These are prepared by the computer system and filled in by the customer before being returned and read directly into the computer system
MICR	This uses magnetic ink, and is used mainly on cheques by banks
Optical character readers	Typed or clearly printed orders could be read directly into the system
Mark sense cards and reader	Readers could post mark sense cards that they filled in with their orders. This would cut down on keyboard entry errors and save time, as well as avoiding the need for verification

Now you need to decide which of these is suitable to improve the system and be clear about how it will bring improvements.

The answer

Use mark sense cards. These could be filled in by customers and passed through a high-speed reader, cutting down on keyboards errors and avoiding the need for the operator to verify the data entry. As for telephone orders, the operator could simply complete a mark sense card and pass it through a reader.

Problem solving tips

- You need to know all about every topic on the course.
- You need to be able to choose between different technologies and select the most suitable to solve your problem.

Now you try

1 A hospital has a computer system installed to monitor patients' pulse and breathing. The software that comes with the system is *interpreted*. What translator would you suggest in order to improve the system? Give your reasons for your choice.

2 You work in a busy office with lots of desktop computers, each one has its own printer and scanner. Your boss asks you to suggest a way to cut the expense of having lots of printers and scanners. Outline your suggestion and give your reasons.

Implications of solutions

Sometimes you will be given solutions to problems then asked to comment on their implications for jobs, training, security, legal matters and costs. Here's an example.

Example

A large insurance company installs a multi-access mainframe computer. At first there are problems. Data is lost, viruses are found in the system, people's personal data is being circulated without their permission.

(a) What can be done to improve security?

(b) What laws are being broken by the breaches in security?

(c) The company installs a set of integrated packages. What effect does this have on the training courses?

(d) When the system was introduced it created lots of jobs involved in designing and installing, as well as operating the system. Describe an example of each type of job.

(e) Staff are concerned that there might be problems with health and safety. How should the management deal with their concerns?

How do you answer this type of question? You need to know all about security measures, the laws such as the Data Protection Act, training, health and safety and the jobs created by computer systems.

They are dealt with in Unit 2 General purpose packages. Once you know about these topics they can be used to answer questions set in a whole range of contexts.

Now you try

Now try answering the question in the example above about the insurance company.

Problem solving tips summary

- Before you begin problem solving you need to have a good knowledge of all the topics on the course.
- You need to read each question carefully.
- Think about the information held in the question before you start to form your answer.
- Pick out the key ideas.
- Think how the key ideas point to the solution.
- You may have to give your reasons for a solving a problem. Don't forget to use the *because* word.
- If the question asks you to set out the steps involved in solving a problem, you have to remember to set them out carefully, in the correct order.
- You need to be able to choose between different technologies and select the most suitable to solve your problem.

If you have worked through all the problems in this section and you follow these tips, you should improve your problem solving skills.

Answers to knowledge checks

Unit 1 Communications and networks

Knowledge check 1 page 5

1 True.

2 Share data, peripherals, communicate across LAN.

3 Any three from:

- To transfer money, to send and receive orders.
- To buy and sell things: e-commerce (see page 139).
- To get information, e.g. researching for a school project using the Internet (see page 12).
- To communicate by email (see page 5).
- To enable people to work together across large distances by, for example, using video-conferencing (see page 15), or by working from home and linking into the network in the office using a phone connection.

4 It can be encrypted.

Credit questions

5 Using a system of IDs and passwords.

6 It controls resources available to clients on the network, e.g. a printer server.

7 A user on a workstation attached to a network.

8 It links your computer to your local area network. It stores data coming into and out of your computer and changes it so that it can travel across the network.

Knowledge check 2 page 14

1

Advantages of using e-mail	*Disadvantages of using e-mail*
Easy to access your mail	You can get lots of junk mail
You can send multiple copies to different people	Your mailbox can get cluttered by lots of multiple copies of mail items
The speed of delivery	E-mail attachments can be a source of viruses
Low cost	

2 The Internet is a worldwide system that uses telecommunications systems to link your computer to other computers and networks and right round the world, making it possible for people to share information and communicate with each other.

3 It is a program that helps you to find your way around the World Wide Web and look at Web pages. It fetches Web pages for you and then displays them on your monitor.

4 Chat, newsgroups, file transfer, www.
5 One that has a browser, a modem installed and is ready to access the Internet.
6 A search engine is actually an on-line database that stores a basic description, and addresses, of lots of Web pages. When you ask the search engine to look for something it searches through its data and sends the results of the search to your browser, which displays them on the monitor.
7 A hyperlink joins Web pages together.
8 A dialup connection uses a modem and an ordinary telephone line to connect you to the Internet.

Credit questions
9 Internet Service Provider.
10 It offers access to the Internet, free e-mail, and space on its servers to mount your Web pages.
11 One example is an Eriksson P800. It is a cross between a palmtop and a phone. It has a range of software, including a browser. It uses mobile phone technology to access the Internet. (By searching on the Internet you will be able to find a more up to date example.)
12 Glasgow AND museum OR art gallery NOT transport. Having multiple conditions in your search helps the search engine to narrow your search down, making it more accurate.

Knowledge check 3 page 18

Credit questions
1 Freeware costs you nothing and you can make and distribute copies as long as you don't change it or sell it. You have to pay for shareware after a 30 day trial period. If you make copies for others they have to pay as well, after their trial period.
2 One backup.
3 You can find them either on an FTP site or on a website that specialises in a wide range of software.
4 Point-to-point connects two stations on a network. Multi-point connects several users in different locations.
5 You can see and talk to other people in the conference as well as share data and display and annotate documents. This means they can conduct business at a distance without the need for travelling.
6 One that enables multiple users to access a main computer simultaneously.
7 They can be used to transmit digital copies of copyrighted music, graphics or films. Networks can be used to invade privacy by, for example, sending junk mail or by hacking into computers with personal details.
8 If people have no access to the information that is stored on the Internet then they will be at a disadvantage when it comes to, for example, education, jobs, buying and selling goods.

Unit 2 General purpose packages

Knowledge Check 1 page 27

1 Word processing, databases, spreadsheets, graphics, presentation and multimedia, Web page creation, desktop publishing, expert systems.
2 They save time, they help us communicate with other people, they help us keep our data accurate and prevent loss of data.

3 (a) Spreadsheet packages are designed to handle numbers. They let us store columns and rows of numbers and enter formulae to add them up, work out averages, etc.

(b) Numbers in a word processing document are often used for numbering pages.

(c) Numbers in a database are used for storing anything you want, such as the number of cds you have or the number of books you own. NB: you have to set up *number fields* in your database (see page 49).

4 (a) Text would be used in a spreadsheet document to label rows, columns or individual cells.

(b) Word processing is designed to handle text. It lets us enter text then do all sorts of things with it (see pages 40–41).

(c) In a graphics file text would be used to label parts of the drawing or diagram.

5 They have to deal with MIDI files, which hold the instructions for making sounds, as well as digital representations of sounds, which are made up of samples of the sound waves, turned into patterns of binary numbers.

6 They store photos digitally and then compress them into files called jpegs to make them smaller.

7 A backup is a copy of your files. It is necessary in case the data gets lost or corrupted.

Credit questions

8 (a) They store and display the animation frame by frame.

(b) They can be very large files.

9 Without being compressed to make it smaller it makes too many demands on the computer's main memory and backing storage, and it take a lot longer to transmit across a network.

10 (a) The advantage of an ASCII file is that it is recognised by virtually all systems and it is a compact code because it does not include formatting information.

(b) The advantage of using RTF is that it includes all the formatting information such as styles and fonts, etc.

Knowledge check 2 page 35

1 Human Computer Interface.

2 Windows Icons Menus Pointer.

3 It is so user friendly because it is easy to get your computer to do what you want simply by using the pointer to select from a menu or to select an icon. Your computer then displays your data or software in the windows, which you can move around and resize if you want.

4 An icon is a small graphic.

5 An icon can be used to represent a file, a folder, a program, or piece of hardware like a printer, a hard disk or a CD drive.

6 This is *part of your software* that you can call up and ask for help on any part of the program you don't understand.

7 (a) It is similar because it is part of your software.

(b) It is different because it demonstrates what to do, takes you through examples, and then sets you exercises.

8 A template has the structure of a document in place with boxes for text, and all the formatting set up. All you have to do is fill in the text.

9 A wizard takes you through the setting up of a chart by showing you a series of windows.

10 A toolbar is a type of menu made up of icons.

Credit questions

11 Customising your HCI involves doing things like adjusting the mouse speed, changing the screen display, or altering the size and shape of your icons.

12 People use shortcuts because, once you have learned how to use them, they are a quicker way of getting things done. Using keyboard shortcuts means you don't have to use a series of menus.

Knowledge check 3 page 39

1 An integrated package combines several applications, such as spreadsheets, graphics, databases and word processing, in one package.

2 They have a common HCI and they make transferring data between applications easy.

3 Because it makes it easier to learn how to use the different applications in the package. Because the icons and menus and commands are similar, once you have learned how to use one package it is quite easy to move onto the next one.

4 You could write the text in a word processing document; use the spreadsheet to hold the grades for all the tests and work out the averages, etc; use the database to hold all the pupils details; use the graphics package to draw diagrams or process photographs; and then transfer all the database, spreadsheet and graphics data to the word processing document before printing it out.

Credit questions

5 You can link documents so that the data in the linked document is automatically updated when you update the data held in the source document.

6 It can save you from having to update documents one by one. All you have to do is update the source document and the updating of the other documents is done for you automatically.

7 If the link between two documents is static then the updating is not automatic. You have to intervene and trigger the updating by selecting from a menu or entering a command. In a dynamic link the updating is done automatically.

8 (a) An advantage is that each application in the integrated suite of packages will have more features than in a single integrated package. For example Microsoft Word, part of the MS Office suite, has many more features than the word processing part of Microsoft Works, a single integrated package.

(b) It will demand more backup storage, main memory and make more demands on the processor because it can run two or more applications at the same time.

Knowledge check 4 page 69

1 People might be worried about getting a sore back from being hunched up in front of a computer; about the heat the computer system produces; about having enough room on their desks for the computer systems; and about getting headaches from the glare coming from the monitors.

2 Adjustable chairs could be bought and new wider desks fitted. Good ventilation could be installed and special screens fitted to cut down on glare.

3 There are two sides to this question. Storing information in computer systems does save on paper. However, people do use their computers to produce quality documents and then like to print out copies of their work.

4 A cost that you meet at the start when you set up your computer system, e.g. the cost of buying the computer, the software and the training.

5 They need to be trained in how to operate the hardware such as the printers, scanners, hard disks and CD writers, as well as how to use the application packages.

Knowledge check 5 page 71

Credit questions

1 There are six listed on page 70, here are four of them; people have the right to know if data is held about them, to see a copy of it, to have it changed if it is not correct, to ask for compensation if it is inaccurate or unauthorised people have accessed the data.

The exceptions are that the data subject does not have the right to see data held on them by the police or security services.

2 The Data Protection Commissioner is in charge of administering the Data Protection Act.

3 The principles are listed on page 70, here are four of them:

- data must be held for the specified purpose described in the Register entry
- data must be accurate and where necessary kept up to date
- data must be relevant and not excessive in relation to the purpose for which it is held
- data must be surrounded by proper security.

4 It is a register that holds details about who holds information on members of the public on their computer system.

5 A data subject is the person who has data held about them on a computer system.

6 A data controller is the person, business or organisation controlling the collection, contents and use of personal data.

Knowledge check 6 page 72

Credit questions

1 It is designed to make hacking into computers and changing or copying the data or software illegal. It also makes planting viruses illegal.

2 A hacker is someone who accesses a computer system without authorisation.

3 A virus is a piece of software that damages a computer system.

4 (a) Use a virus checker that will monitor all data coming into your system and prevent viruses getting in.

(b) You can recover files from the backup copies that have been made.

5 You can set passwords and encode the data.

6 You can have locks on the computer room, locks on the computer terminals, and you can have workstations without disk drives.

7 It is designed to make it illegal to copy software without permission, to run illegal copies of software, and to transmit illegal copies across a network.

Unit 3 Automated systems

Knowledge check 1 page 80

1 They can operate at high speeds, they can handle repetitive tasks, they are accurate, they work in dangerous places, and they are adaptable.

2 A stationary robot is fixed in one place, it is usually a robot arm.

3 Any one from: welding, spray painting, lifting parts.

4 Carrying heavy loads around a factory, or dangerous materials such as chemicals.
5 A light is shone onto the floor and is reflected off a white line. Sensors on each side of the robot detect the light being reflected and send that data to the processor which sends out signals to control the motors.
6 A CAD system has a high resolution monitor, a powerful processor and lots of backing storage.
7 CAM is Computer Aided Manufacture, the use of computers to control machinery in factories.
8 A spray gun, welding tool, gripper, suction pad, magnetic tool for lifting metal, specialised tools for factory assembly.

Credit question

9 Automated systems are adaptable because they can be re-programmed to carry out another job. If the automated system has a robot arm, the tool can be changed.

Knowledge check 2 page 85

1 Control language.
2 Sensors collect the data that is then fed back to the processor.
3 Humidity sensors – used to control humidity levels in a greenhouse; heat sensors – used as part of an alarm system; light sensors – used as part of the guidance system for a mobile robot; pressure sensors – used to monitor pressures in an oil refinery.
4 The job of an interface is to translate the signals coming into a computer system into the digital form that the processor can understand and, vice versa, to enable the computer to communicate with the machinery it is controlling.
5 Automated systems have to react instantly, e.g. a system controlling a robot arm must react to data from its sensors instantly.
6 Simulation is the use of a computer based system to mimic something in the real world. They can be used for training purposes, e.g. learning to fly a plane.

Credit questions

7 An A/D converter changes the analogue signals coming in, e.g. from a sensor, into digital data. It does so by sampling the analogue signal thousands of times each second then converting the samples into digital numbers before sending them onto the processor.
8 An embedded system is a machine that has its own microchip and memory attached to it, for control purposes.
9 An intelligent robot is one which has its own processor and memory and which has sensors attached to it which give it human like capabilities e.g. hearing or seeing.
10
- Optical sensors to 'see' objects.
- Sonar beams and sensors to navigate, rather like a bat.
- Tactile sensors in the base so that it can detect the different types of surface it is travelling over, e.g. carpets, wooden floors.
- Microphones and a voice recognition system to take in commands.

Knowledge check 3 page 87

1 Because large sums of money need to be invested in equipment before the work can even begin.
2 Initial costs – the computers, the software, the robots, the systems analysts.
Running costs – staff wages, electricity bills, maintenance of robots.

3 Because they are accurate and can handle repetitive tasks at high speeds without making mistakes, they will produce high quality goods quickly and they cut down on waste as well as wages.

4 Safety signs could be hung around the factory, areas on the floor on which the robots travel could be painted bright yellow, sirens and 'bump' sensors could be fitted onto mobile robots.

5 Systems analyst, installation and maintenance engineers, operators.

Credit questions

6 The systems analyst would decide what jobs the robots had to do, what the layout of the factory would look like and which of the following would need to be installed:

- Sensors
- A guidance system
- Power cables and data cables
- A controlling computer system
- Safety systems

7 Paths must be marked for mobile robots, areas where stationary robots work must be set aside, safety measures must be introduced to protect people, cabling and sensors need to be installed.

Unit 4 Computer systems

Knowledge check 1 page 93

1 Machine code is the language the computer really understands. It is made up of 1s and 0s, e.g. 11100111.

2 (a) English.
(b) Solve problems.

3

Interpreter	It translates each line one at a time every time the program runs
Compiler	It translates high-level language instructions into machine code once only
Interpreter	It points out the syntax errors as you write the program
Compiler	Using this translator your program written in a high-level language runs faster because it is only translated once
Compiler	This translator shows you your errors after you have entered all your coding in a high-level language and try to translate the program

Knowledge check 2 page 100

1 An operating system is a program that controls all the tasks your computer carries out like opening files, saving files to disk, reading in data from the keyboard and storing data in memory.

2 How about your word processor application and your database application for the program files, and a word processing file and a database file for your data files?

3 They are used for storing files and other folders. They help you organise your files and folders.

4 It processes each job and updates files immediately within a second or two. Real time processing often involves sensors feeding in data, which the processor reacts to in a fraction of a second, much faster than an interactive system. Real time processing is used to control machines (see Unit 3 Automated systems).

5 (a) Interactive processing.
(b) Real time processing.
(c) Interactive processing.

Credit questions

6 A bank that allows account data files to be updated interactively while, at quiet times, prints out customer account statements in the background.

7 Files are kept on different levels in directories and sub-directories (folders).

8 It helps you keep your files in a logical order and so it is easier to locate files. It is also easier to manage access to files by setting access privileges to certain folders.

9 The system starts at the beginning of the sequence and reads each piece of data in turn until it locates what it needs.

10 Because a tape is sequential. The tape drive starts at the beginning of a tape and reads each part of the tape until it reaches the end.

11 It goes directly to the data it requires, unlike sequential access, which has to look at each item in the sequence in turn until it finds the data it wants.

12 Any two from: hard disks, CD ROMs, CD-RW and DVDs.

Knowledge check 3 page 103

1 The 'brains' of a computer system.

2 Input, Process, Output.

3 (a) Read only.
(b) It is cleared.

4

8 Bits	1 Byte
1024 Megabytes	1 Gbyte
1024 Bytes	1 Kbyte
1024 Kilobytes	1 Mbyte
1024 Gigabytes	1 Terabyte

Credit question

5

Register	The processor uses this to store data, instructions and addresses
ALU and CU	These are two parts of the CPU
Memory location	Each of these has its own address
CU	This sends out signals to fetch instructions and carry them out
Comparing two values	This is an example of a *Logic* operation

Knowledge check 4 page 104

1 Binary, 0s.

2

1000001 =	65
1000010 =	66
1000011 =	67
1000100 =	68

Credit question

3

2^7	2^6	2^5	2^4	2^3	2^2	2^1	2^0	Power of 2
128	64	32	16	8	4	2	1	Decimal
0	1	0	1	0	1	0	1	Binary

64 + 16 + 4 + 1 = 85

Knowledge check 5 page 107

1 American Standard Code for Information Interchange.

2 Binary number.

3 (a) 1000001 = 65
(b) 1000010 = 66
(c) 1000011 = 67

4

A point on the screen is a	Pixel
In a black and white drawing each pixel is represented by	1 or a 0
The storage needed for a black and white graphic 8 pixels × 8 pixels is	64 bits

Knowledge check 6 page 108

1 Floppy disk, hard disk, tape.

2 (a)

This holds 1.44 Mbytes	Floppy disk
In today's PCs these hold 100+ gigabytes	Hard disk
One of these cartridges holds several gigabytes	Dat tape

(b)

They are useful when transferring small files to another computer	Floppy disk
They are used as the main backing storage on most computers	Hard disk
They are used to make backups	Tapes
They are usually sealed inside your computer to keep them free from dust	Hard disks
They are very cheap and cost only a few pence	Floppy disks

Knowledge check 7 page 110

1 (a) CD-ROM
(b) 650 Mbytes of data.
(c) Reading light reflected off the surface of the disk.
(d) CD-ROM
(e) CD-RW
(f) DVD

2

Statement	*True/false*
A USB flash drive is a memory chip	True
You can store data on it and then change it	True
You can unplug it from the computer and put it in your pocket	True
It holds the same amount of data as a floppy disc	False
When you unplug it from the computer it loses data	False

3 You would need to use a USB flash drive because it has enough capacity and is removable, so you can take it to friend's house and attach it to his computer.

Knowledge check 8 page 116

1 You would most likely use a mouse to control the pointer then click to make your selection.

2 (a) Graphics tablet
(b) Trackball
(c) Keyboard
(d) Scanner
(e) Sound card
(f) Gloves with sensors attached
(g) Touch-sensitive screen
(h) Digital camera
(i) Microphone

Knowledge check 9 page 121

1 (a) Laser printer
(b) Monitor
(c) Inkjet
(d) LCD screens
(e) Voice output
(f) Plotter

2 (a) It is small enough to fit on your hand or in your pocket; it has a small keyboard; it stores its data on a *flashcard*; it can be used for storing appointments and for simple word processing and spreadsheet tasks; it is powered by a small battery.
(b) It is small and compact: you can carry it about easily; it is light (it weighs 3–4 kg); it uses re-chargeable batteries or mains power.
(c) It is made up of a monitor, a keyboard and mouse and the casing, which holds the processor, the memory and the disk drives; it fits neatly onto a desk; it often has peripherals attached, such as a scanner or printer.

3 You can use it as a personal organiser, as a portable electronic diary, or you can even takes notes on it or store information in its database.

4. Laptops are portable and have all the functionality of a desktop. They are very useful when travelling between offices and can be used to prepare and show presentations. Equipped with a modem they can easily be connected to the Internet.
5. A desktop has a good monitor, powerful processor and lots of backing storage. You can also connect large peripherals like a scanner and a printer.

Credit questions

6. Your report should contain the latest examples of sound cards. It should have info about the sampling rates available, the number of bits per sample and the number of channels it offers (this affects the number of speakers it can drive).
7. Having a processor on board the graphics card relieves the main processor of the burden of handling all the complex graphics.

Knowledge check 10 page 124

Credit questions

1. Multimedia systems incorporate and integrate sound, animated images, video and graphics within a single user-friendly computer interface.
2. - To provide interactive learning systems where the learner can interact with and access text, video images, sound tracks and graphics.
   - For interactive information systems.
   - For displaying multimedia web pages.
   - For games.
3. Here is an example of a multimedia computer at the time of writing. By the time you read this, this will be out of date and you will need to update it by looking in the latest magazines.
   - A fast processor: 2 GHZ and above.
   - 512+ Mbytes of RAM.
   - A 60 Gbyte+ hard disc.
   - A 42 speed CD-ROM.
   - A CD /DVD writer.
   - Sound and graphics interfaces.
   - A set of speakers.
   - A good quality monitor.
4. Ultrasound transmitters that pinpoint the user's movements. Strips that vary their resistance when bent.
5. In gloves, suits and helmets.
6. A pair of miniature high quality screens produce a realistic 3-dimensional environment. A pair of high quality speakers produce all round sound.
7. The output is so effective that the user is convinced he or she is inside the computer's world.
8. The job of a sound card is to change the samples of the sound wave into digital numbers so that the computer can store and process them. When the computer is sending sound data to the speakers the sound card has to reverse the process and turn the digital sound data into analogue signals to control the speaker output.
9. Any two from: eye sensors, head tracking mouse, specialised keyboards, touchpad and touch-sensitive screens.

Knowledge check 1 page 132

1 A bank, a mail order company, a payroll system in a factory.
2 They can cope with high volumes of data; they handle repetitive work easily; they process data at high speed; they are very accurate and eliminate mistakes, providing all data is input correctly (see page 128 for other reasons).
3 Information is data that has been processed and has some meaning and structure.

4

The first stage of the data processing cycle	Collecting, preparing and entering the data
Magnetised ink, used on cheques and read into the computer by a special reader	MICR
Magnetic stripe on the back of a card, holding account details.	Magnetic stripes
Pen or pencil marks on a card can be read as data into a computer	Mark sense card
Black and white lines which represent numbers.	Bar code

5 Optical character reader.
6 Smart card.

Knowledge check 2 page 134

1

Checking that numbers and characters have been entered in the correct places	Field type check
Checking that the entry is not too big for the field.	Field length check
Checking that the entry is in a specified range (e.g. 1 to 100)	Field range check
The computer calculates this number in order to make sure that the other numbers in a sequence have been entered properly	Check digit
Checks to make sure that an entry has been made into a field	Presence check

Credit questions

2 When data is entered at a keyboard by an operator, it is checked to make sure that it has been entered correctly. For example either the operator checks data on screen before entering it in to the system, or two operators enter data, which the computer then compares for differences.

3 Verification is usually carried out by the operator at the keyboard when he/she checks the data displayed on the screen. It checks that the data has been entered correctly from the form or telephone call. Validation is carried out by a program running in the computer, which checks that all the data has been entered in the correct places.

Knowledge check 3 page 137

1 (a) Records.
(b) Fields.
(c) Items of data.
(d) Interactive processing *updates* the data files *immediately*. It is used by banks to update files after people withdraw money from cashpoints.

2 Regular backups are made to ensure that systems can recover their data if it is corrupted or lost.

3 System security: IDs and passwords, encryption of data, and using smartcards or auditing software.
Other security measures: fitting each computer terminal with a lock and key, using security locks on doors to computer rooms, using terminals without floppy or CD drives to make it more difficult for viruses to be transferred and data copied.

4 Because all of the customers will be billed, so the computer has to access each one in turn, in sequence.

5 Because when a customer requests a withdrawal the bank's computer needs to access their account data *instantly* to find out if they have enough money to cover the withdrawal. It needs to go directly to the data it needs.

6 A multi-user database is needed. Because of the large volume of transactions involved the system will need to have a database management system with client software available for each of the users and server software managing the transactions, probably mounted on a dedicated server.

Knowledge check 4 page 141

1 Monitors are used to *display* the *data* on the computer system.

2 They are used to produce large numbers of documents such as account statements very quickly.

3 Mainframes can have many terminals attached to them. They have very fast processors; they have a large internal memory; and they have lots of backing storage.

4

Systems analysts	Work out the tasks that the CDP System has to carry out Decide on the hardware that is needed *Design the software* Make sure the system is set up and tested correctly
Programmers	Programmers write the *software* that runs the CDP Systems.
Engineers	Engineers *set up* the hardware and do any *maintenace* that is needed – e.g. repairing disk drives
Network managers	Set up user IDs, *control access* to files, set up links to *printers*, install software, control access to *websites* on the Internet

5 It uses computer systems to transfer money from one bank account to another, e.g. from a customer's account to the supermarket's.

6 Advantage for the customers: they get a better service, the shelves are fully stocked, the checkout is much quicker, receipts have all the details and there are fewer mistakes.

7 In a supermarket or a large store.

8 Advantage for the store: The scanning system keeps a record of everything the store has sold each day. This means that the shelves can be well stocked and the business can keep an up to date record of all the money coming in at the tills.

9 Check balance, make transfers, pay bills, arrange an overdraft, check out mortgage and loan deals.

10 E-commerce is a way of using the Internet to buy and sell goods.

11 The customer can view, order and pay for the goods at home, then have them delivered to the door.

12 Initial costs are one-off costs that you have to meet when you start up a system, e.g. buying the computers and printers. Running costs are always there, e.g. staff wages and electricity bills.

How to analyse your score

Unit 1 Communications and networks

End of unit progress check

How did you get on in the end of unit progress check?

If you scored **more than 21**, then you have done well and are working at credit level. If you scored **above 27** you are doing very well indeed at credit level. If you got any wrong, make sure you have copied out the correct answers before moving on.

If you scored **between 11 and 20** you are working at general level. If you want to, you can re-read all the credit parts of the unit then do the credit questions again.

If you scored **below 11** you are working at foundation level. If you want to, you can re-read all the foundation/general parts of the unit then do the foundation/general questions again.

Unit 2 General-purpose packages

Mid-unit progress check

How did you get on in the mid-unit progress check on application packages?

If you scored **more than 35** then you have done well and are working at credit level. If you scored **above 50** you are doing very well indeed at credit level. If you got any wrong, make sure you have copied out the correct answers before moving on.

If you scored **between 19 and 34** you are working at general level. If you want to you can re-read all the credit parts of the unit then do the credit questions again.

If you scored **below 19** you are working at foundation level. If you want to, you can re-read all the foundation/general parts of the unit then do the foundation/general questions again.

End of unit progress check

How did you get on in the end of unit progress check?

If you scored **more than 20** then you have done well and are working at credit level. If you scored **above 27** you are doing very well indeed at credit level. If you got any wrong, make sure you have copied out the correct answers before moving on.

If you scored **between 11 and 18** you are working at general level. If you want to you can re-read all the credit parts of the unit then do the credit questions again.

If you scored **below 11** you are working at foundation level. If you want to, you can re-read all the foundation/general parts of the unit then do the foundation/general questions again.

Unit 3 Automated systems

End of unit progress check

How did you get on in the end of unit progress check?

If you scored **more than 22** then you have done well and are working at credit level. If you scored **above 28** you are doing very well indeed at credit level. If you got any wrong, make sure you have copied out the correct answers before moving on.

If you scored **between 12 and 22** you are working at general level. If you want to, you can re-read all the credit parts of the unit then do the credit questions again.

If you scored **below 12** you are working at foundation level. If you want to, you can re-read all the foundation/general parts of the unit then do the foundation/general questions again.

Unit 4 Computer systems

End of unit progress check

How did you get on in the end of unit progress check?

If you scored **more than 17** then you have done well and are working at credit level. If you scored **above 29** you are doing very well indeed at credit level. If you got any wrong, make sure you have copied out the correct answers before moving on.

If you scored **between 8 and 17** you are working at general level. If you want to, you can re-read all the credit parts of the unit then do the credit questions again.

If you scored **less than 8** you are working at foundation level. If you want to, you can re-read all the foundation/general parts of the unit then do the foundation/general questions again.

Unit 5 Commercial data processing

End of unit progress check

How did you get on in the end of unit progress check?

If you scored **more than 19**, then you have done well and are working at credit level. If you scored **above 28** you are doing very well indeed at credit level. If you got any wrong, make sure you have copied out the correct answers before moving on.

If you scored **between 10 and 21** you are working at general level. If you want to, you can re-read all the credit parts of the unit then do the credit questions again.

If you scored **below 10** you are working at foundation level. If you want to, you can re-read all the foundation/general parts of the unit then do the foundation/general questions again.

Index